The Case for Anthroposophy

Published by Barfield Press

Books by Owen Barfield:

Eager Spring
Night Operation
The Rose on the Ash-Heap
Poetic Diction: A Study in Meaning
This Ever Diverse Pair
Worlds Apart: A Dialogue of the 1960's
Unancestral Voice

Translations:

The Case for Anthroposophy

Forthcoming new editions:

The Silver Trumpet
Orpheus: A Poetic Drama
English People
Short stories
Poetry

www.owenbarfield.org

The Case for Anthroposophy

being extracts from
Von Seelenrätseln
(Riddles of the Soul)
by
Rudolf Steiner

Selected, translated, arranged,
and with an Introduction by Owen Barfield

Barfield Press
OXFORD, ENGLAND

Copyright © 2010 Owen Barfield Literary Estate

All images are privately owned.

The right of Owen Barfield to be identified as the author of the introduction to this work has been asserted in accordance with the Copyright, Designs and Patents Act 1988.

All rights reserved. No part of this publication may be reproduced, stored in a retrieval system, or transmitted in any form or by any means, electronic, mechanical, photocopying, recording or otherwise without permission in writing from the Owen Barfield Literary Estate.

Series Editor: Dr. Jane Hipolito

Published by Barfield Press UK
Oxford, England

First published by Rudolph Steiner Press, London 1970
This Second Edition, Oxford 2010

A catalogue record for this book is available from the British Library.

The Case for Anthroposophy
translation by Owen Barfield
ISBN 978-0-9559582-3-6

Printed on paper with Sustainable Forestry Initiative (SFI) accreditation.

Produced on behalf of
the Owen Barfield Literary Estate.

The Literary Estate promotes and safeguards the works
and intellectual legacy of Arthur Owen Barfield.

O B

www.owenbarfield.org

CONTENTS

	INTRODUCTION by Owen Barfield	1
I	ANTHROPOLOGY AND ANTHROPOSOPHY	19
II	THE PHILOSOPHICAL BEARING OF ANTHROPOSOPHY	41
III	CONCERNING THE LIMITS OF KNOWLEDGE	49
IV	CONCERNING ABSTRACTION	53
V	CONCERNING THE NATURE OF SPIRITUAL PERCEPTION	57
VI	REPLY TO A FAVOURITE OBJECTION	59
VII	PRINCIPLES OF PSYCHOSOMATIC PHYSIOLOGY	63
VIII	THE REAL BASIS OF INTENTIONAL RELATION	79
	BIBLIOGRAPHY	86
	INDEX	88

INTRODUCTION
by Owen Barfield

THE PROLONGED HISTORICAL event now usually referred to as "the scientific revolution" was characterised by the appearance of a new attitude to the element of sense perception in the total human experience. At first as an instinct, then as a waxing habit, and finally as a matter of deliberate choice, it came to be accepted that this element is, for the purposes of knowledge, the only reliable one; and further that it is possible, and indeed necessary, to isolate, in a way that had not hitherto been thought possible, this one element from all the others that go to make up man's actual experience of the world. The word "matter" came to signify, in effect, that which the senses can, or could, perceive without help from the mind, or from any other source not itself perceptible by the senses.

Whereas hitherto the perceptible and the imperceptible had been felt as happily intermixed with one another, and had been explored on that footing, the philosopher Descartes finally formulated the insulation of matter from mind as a philosophical principle, and the methodology of natural science is erected on that principle. It was by the rigorous exclusion from its field, under the name of "occult qualities", of every element, whether spiritual or mental or called by any other name, which can only be conceived as non-material, and therefore non-measurable, that natural knowledge acquired a precision unknown before the revolution — because inherently impossible in terms of the old fusion; and, armed with that precision (entitling it to the name of "science"), went on to achieve its formidable technological victories. It is the elimination of occult qualities from the purview of science that constitutes the difference between astrology and astronomy, between alchemy and chemistry, and in general the difference between Aristotelian man and his environment in the past and modern man and his environment in the present.

When two mutually dependent human relatives are separated, so that, for the first time, one of them can "go it alone", there may be drawbacks, but it is the advantages that are often most immediately evident. By freeing itself from the taint of "occult qualities", that is, by meticulously disentangling itself from all reference, explicit or implicit, to non-material factors, the material world, as a field of knowledge, gained inestimable advantages. We perhaps take them for granted now; but the men of the seventeenth century — the members of the Royal Society for instance — had a prophetic inkling of what the new liberty promised. You have only to read some of their pronouncements. For them it was an emotional as well as an intellectual experience. "Bliss was it in that dawn to be alive ..."

But when two people separate, so that one of them can go it alone, it follows as a natural consequence that the other can also go it alone. It might have been expected, then, that, by meticulously disentangling itself from all reference, explicit or implicit, to material factors, the *immaterial*, as a field of knowledge, would also gain inestimable advantages. That is what did not happen. But it will be well to state at once that it is nevertheless precisely this *correlative* epistemological principle that is the basis of Rudolf Steiner's anthroposophy. It belongs to the post-Aristotelian age for the same reason that natural science does; but in the opposite way. Thus, the parallel terms, "spiritual science" and "occult science", which he also used, do *not* betoken a fond belief that the methodology of technological[1] science can be applied to the immaterial. The methodology of technological science is, rightly, based on the exclusion of *all* occult qualities from its thinking. The methodology of spiritual science is based on an equally rigorous exclusion of *all* "physical qualities" from its thinking. That is one of the things I hope this book will help to make clear.

What did happen was well expressed by Samuel Taylor Coleridge, when he pointed out in his *Aids to Reflection* that Descartes, having discovered a technical principle, which "as a fiction of science, it would be difficult to overvalue", erroneously propounded that principle as a truth of fact. (The principle in question was the necessity of abstracting from corporeal substance all its positive properties, "in order to submit the various *phaenomena* of moving bodies to geometrical construction".) And of course the same point has since been made by A. N. Whitehead and others.

---

[1] The use of this word is not intended to imply that science, as we have it, is valuable only for the purpose of technical manipulation and construction. It does imply that its cognitive value, as "natural" science, is limited to the extent to which nature is governed by physical laws. The fond belief referred to is of course the assumption underlying the "favourite objection", to which Section VI replies.

But Coleridge could also point prophetically, in another place,[2] to

> the necessity of a general revolution in the modes of developing and disciplining the human mind by the substitution of Life, and Intelligence (considered in its different powers from the Plant up to that state in which the difference of Degree becomes a new kind — man, self-consciousness — but yet not by essential opposition) for the philosophy of mechanism which in everything that is most worthy of the human Intellect strikes *Death*, and cheats itself by mistaking clear Images for distinct conceptions ...

The necessity for such a revolution, he said, arises from the fact that, for self-conscious man, although to experience a world of corporeal substance as existing quite apart from his thinking self is "a law of his nature," it is *not* "a conclusion of his judgment". That this is indeed the case hardly needs arguing today, since it has become the discovery of technological science itself. Whether we go to neurology or to physics, or elsewhere, we are confronted with the demonstrable conclusion that the actual, macroscopic world of nature — as distinct from the microscopic, submicroscopic and inferred world of physical science — is (as, for instance, the biologist, Professor Marjorie Grene, puts it in her book *The Knower and the Known*) "mediated by concepts as well as presented through the senses". What is remarkable is the rapidity with which the presence of this Trojan Horse in the citadel of its methodology was detected by technological science

---

[2] Letter to William Wordsworth, 30 May 1815.

itself, as it was progressively realised that everything in nature that constitutes her "qualities" must be located on the *res cogitans*, and not the *res extensa*, side of the Cartesian guillotine. But this is as much as to say that those qualities are, in the technological sense, "occult"; and it could be argued without much difficulty that any science which proposes to enquire into them must also be "occult" — unless it is content to do so by extrapolating into the psyche a theoretical apparatus applicable, by definition, *only* to subject-matter that has first been sedulously dehydrated of *all* psyche. Yet this last is the approach which the methodology of natural science, as we have it, renders inevitable. If you have first affirmed that the material world is in fact independent of the psychic, and then determined to concentrate attention exclusively on the former, it does not make all that difference whether or no you go to the behaviouristic lengths of explicitly denying the existence of psyche. Either it does not exist or, if it does exist, it is occult and must be left severely alone. In any case you have withdrawn attention from it for so long that it might as well not be there, as far as you are concerned. For the purpose of cognition, it will gradually (as the author puts it on page 70) "peter out".

Moreover this continues to be the case even after the failure of science to eliminate psyche from the knowable world has become evident. The demonstrative arguments of a Coleridge, a Whitehead, a Michael Polanyi are perforce acknowledged; but the acknowledgment remains an intellectual, not an emotional experience. The Trojan Horse certainly does seem to be there, and in rather a conspicuous way; but the necessary traffic-diversions can be arranged, and it is much less embarrassing to leave it standing in the market-place than to get involved.

There is however one experience inseparable from the progress of natural science, which is apt to be an emotional as well as an intellectual one. And that is the fact that the exclusion of the psychic, as such, from matter of science entails recognition of the *limits* of science. This is, of course, the opposite experience from the one that enthralled the scientists of the seventeenth century. They rejoiced in a conviction that all the boundaries had gone and the prospects opened up to human knowledge had become limitless. Whereas, more and more as the nineteenth century progressed, it was the opposite that was stressed. "Ignorabimus." We shall *never* know. There are limits beyond which, in the very nature of things, the mind can never pass. One of the things heavily stressed by Steiner (in Section I and again more specifically in Section III) is the significance, from the point of view of anthroposophy, of precisely this experience, and not so much in itself as for what it may lead to. The more monstrous and menacing the Horse is felt to be, towering there and casting its shadow over the centre of the town, the more ready we may be to begin asking ourselves whether there may not perhaps be something alive inside it.

This experience can be an emotional, and indeed a volitional one, because it involves a frustrating, if suppressed, conflict between the scientific *impulse*, which is a will to know and a refusal to acknowledge boundaries except for the purpose of overthrowing them — and the scientific *tradition*, followed for the last three hundred years, which has ended in itself erecting boundaries that claim to be no less absolute than the old theological ones it did overthrow.

In developing his contention that the shock of contact with these self-imposed limits of knowledge may itself be the necessary first step towards breaching them, the author refers in particular to two German writers, F. T. Vischer and Gideon Spicker. It would be a mistake to conclude from this, or from the nineteenth century idiom of the quotations, that the theme is out of date. The boundaries are still there and are still felt. The substance is the same, whether it is Gideon Spicker pointing out that

> every one, without exception, starts from an unproven and unprovable premise, namely the *necessity of thinking*. No investigation ever gets behind this necessity, however deep it may dig. It has to be simply and groundlessly accepted ...

or Bertrand Russell, in *Human Knowledge: Its Scope and Limits*, conceding that the foundation, on which the whole structure of empirical science is erected, is itself demonstrably non-empirical:

> If an individual is to know anything beyond his own experiences up to the present moment, his stock of uninferred knowledge must consist not only of matters of fact, but also of general laws, or at least a law, allowing him to make inferences from matters of fact ... The only alternative to this hypothesis is complete scepticism as to all the inferences of science and common sense, including those which I have called animal inference.

The abiding question is, how we choose to react to the boundaries. We may, with Russell and the empiricists, having once conscientiously "shown awareness" of them, proceed henceforth to ignore them and hope, so to speak, that they will go away; or, with the linguistic philosophers, we may flatly decline to look at them; or we may wrap ourselves in the vatic "silence" of a Heidegger or a Wittgenstein or a Norman O. Brown to be broken only by paradox and aphorism, or fall in behind the growing number of distinguished enthusiasts for metaphor, symbol and myth; or, with the scientific positivists, we may resign ourselves to the conviction that there is really no difference between knowledge and technology; we may even perhaps attempt some new definition of knowledge along the lines of the groping relativism, or personalism, of Karl Popper or of Michael Polanyi. But how far all of these are from the vision that was engendered by the scientific impulse in its first appearance among men! Steiner, as will be seen, advocates a different response, and one which, it seems to me, is more in accord with the fateful impulse itself, however it may differ from the methodology and the tradition which that impulse has so far begotten.

At intervals through the ensuing pages the reader will encounter a passing reference to, and sometimes a quotation from, the German philosopher and psychologist, Franz Brentano. Here too he may be inclined to form a hasty judgment that the book is unduly "dated" by them. But here too it is the substance that matters, and that is far from being out of date. What that substance is, it is hoped, may be sufficiently gathered from the book itself. Brentano is however so little known to English readers that I have thought it best to omit from the translation that part of it which amounts to an exegesis of his psychology. There remain two points to which I wish to draw attention here. In a short section entitled "Diremption of the Psychic from the Extra-psychic in Brentano" (also omitted) the author briefly capitulates the former's refutation of a certain influential and still widely accepted psychological fallacy: namely, that the degree of conviction with which we treat a proposition as "true" (and thus, the existential component in any existential judgment) depends on the degree of intensity — the "passion"[3] with which we *feel* it. This, says Brentano, is based on an impermissible analogy ("size") between the psyche itself on the one hand and the world of space on the other. If conviction really depended on intensity of feeling, doctors would be advising their patients against studying mathematics, or even learning arithmetic, for fear of a nervous breakdown. What it in fact depends on, adds Steiner, is an inner intuition of the psyche neither similar nor analogous, but *corresponding in its objectivity*, to the psyche's outer experience of causality in the physical world. And this experience is considered elsewhere in the book, for instance in Sections VII and VIII.

The other point concerns Brentano's relation to the present day. It is not always the philosopher whose name is best known and whose works are still read, whose influence is most abiding. Brentano was the teacher of Edmund Husserl, who acknowledged that teaching as the

---

[3] Polanyi's word.

determining influence in his intellectual and vocational life; and without the Phenomenology of Husserl, with its stress on the "intentionality" or "intentional relation" in the act of perceiving, there is some doubt whether Existentialism would ever have been born. Thus, while from a superficial point of view the relation to Brentano, which certainly pervades the book as a whole, may be felt as a dating one, for anyone at all acquainted in detail with the history of western thought it can have the consequence of bringing it almost modishly up to date.

Steiner's *Von Seelenrätseln* (of which what follows is a partial translation) is not a systematic presentation of the philosophical basis of anthroposophy. For that the reader must go to his *The Philosophy of Freedom*, or *Goethe's Theory of Knowledge*, or *Truth and Science*;[4] and perhaps especially the last. The Foreword to *Von Seelenrätseln* does in fact describe it as a *Rechtfertigung* — vindication — of anthroposophical methodology, but my choice of a title for these extracts came from the impression I had myself retained of its essential content after reading the whole and translating a good deal of it. Steiner's *Von Seelenrätseln* was published in 1917, the year of Brentano's death; and its longest section (here omitted) amounts, as its title, *Franz Brentano (Ein Nachruf)*, suggests, to an obituary essay. Steiner had always, he says in a Foreword, been both an admirer and an assiduous reader of Brentano and had long been intending to write about him. The main body of the

---

[4] See Bibliography.

essay is thus a patient and detailed exposition, supported by quotations, of Brentano's psychology, in which the word "judgment" is used to name that intentional relation between the psyche and the extra-psychic, or physical world, which enables it either to reject a representation as subjective or to accept it as objective. This "judgment" is an exclusively psychic activity, and must be sharply distinguished as such from both representations and feelings. As the essay proceeds, Steiner makes it clear that he sees Brentano's emphasis on intentionality as a first step in the direction of that psychological elimination of "physical qualities", to which I have already referred. And he suggests that the only reason why Brentano himself could not take the logically indicated second step (which must have carried him in the direction of anthroposophy) was that at the very outset of his philosophical career, following Emmanuel Kant, he had irrevocably nailed his colours to the back of the Cartesian guillotine, by accepting the axiom that concepts without sensory content are "empty". Is this why today, although we have a philosophical and an ethical existentialism, and now even an existential psychology, we have as yet no existential epistemology?

This essay is immediately preceded by a lengthy response in detail to a chapter in a then recently published book by Max Dessoir, and that in its turn by the introductory essay entitled *Anthropology and Anthroposophy*, which also forms the opening section of the book now presented to English readers. The arguments against including *Max Dessoir über Anthroposophie* seemed to me to be the same, only a good deal stronger than those against including the Brentano obituary. Steiner felt bound to go into Dessoir's chapter in some detail, because it echoed irresponsibly a number of flagrant misunderstandings, or misrepresentations, of anthroposophy that were current in Germany at the time. Briefly, Dessoir's arguments are all based on the assumption that anthroposophy ignores the principles of natural science and must collapse as soon as it is confronted with them; whereas Steiner's real argument is, as he himself formulates it in the Foreword, that "either the grounds for there being such a thing as anthroposophy are valid, or else no truth-value can be assigned to the insights of natural science itself". What he disputed was not facts, but hypotheses which have come to be treated as facts. I have omitted the Foreword; but the argument, so formulated, is sufficiently apparent from the rest of the book.

The remainder of *Von Seelenrätseln* consists of eight Commentary Notes (*Skizzenhafte Erweiterungen*) of varying lengths, each referring specifically to a different point in the text, but each bearing a title and all of them quite capable, it seems to me, of standing on their own. Seven of them appear here as Sections II to VIII, and I have already borrowed from the eighth (*Diremption of the Psychic from the Extra-psychic in Brentano*) for the purposes of this Introduction.

We are left with a book rather less than half the length of the original and requiring, if only for that reason, a different title; but still with a book which I have thought it important to make available, as best I can, in the English tongue; and that not only for the general reasons I have already suggested, but also for a particular one with which I will conclude.

One of the Commentary Notes (Section VII) stands on rather a different footing, is perhaps even in a different category, from the others. At a certain point in the Brentano obituary Steiner quotes from a previous book of his own a passage in which he compares the relation between the unconscious and the conscious psyche to that between a man himself and his reflection in a looking-glass. In which case the notion that the actual *life* of the soul consists of the way it expresses itself through the body, would be as fantastic as that of a man, regarding himself in a mirror, who should suppose that the form he sees there has been produced by the mirror. Whereas of course the mirror is the condition, not the cause, of what he sees. In the same way, the ordinary waking experience of the psyche certainly is conditioned by its bodily apparatus; but "it is not the soul itself that is dependent on the bodily instruments, but only the *ordinary consciousness* of the soul". Now Section VII is, in form, a Note on this sentence; and it is somewhat odd that Steiner should have chosen a "Note" for the purpose to which he applied it. For he made it the occasion of his first mention (after thirty years of silent reflection and study) of the principle of psychosomatic triunity. Moreover it is still the *locus classicus* for a full statement of that same "threefold" principle, which, as every serious student of it knows, lies at the very foundation of anthroposophy, while at the same time it runs like a twisted Ariadne's thread through nearly every matter selected for scrutiny. Even those readers, therefore, who are already too well convinced to feel that any "case" for anthroposophy is needed so far as they are concerned, will probably be glad to have it available in book form and in the English language. It has once before been translated — in 1925 by the late George Adams — but his version was only printed in a privately circulated periodical and has been out of print for many years.

It hardly needs adding that this Note in particular will repay particularly careful study. But there is one aspect of it, and of the doctrine it propounds, to which I feel impelled to direct attention before I withdraw and leave the book to speak for itself. If Section I is the statement, Section VII strikes me as a particularly good *illustration*, of the true relation between Steiner's anthroposophy and that natural science which the scientific revolution has in fact brought about. Although he criticises, and rejects, a certain conclusion which has been drawn from the evidence afforded by neurological experiments, Steiner does not attack the physiology developed since Harvey's day; still less does he ignore it; he enlists it. It is not only psychologically (for the reason already given) but also technologically that the scientific revolution was a necessary precondition of anthroposophical cognition. And this has a bearing on an objection of a very different order that is sometimes brought against it. I was myself once asked: What is there in Steiner that you do not also find in Jacob Boehme, if you know how to look for it?

The content of Section VII (here called "Principles of Psychosomatic Physiology") could never have come to light in the context of an Aristotelian physiology, a physiology of "animal spirits", for example, and of four "elements" that were psychic as well as physical and four "humours" that were physical as well as psychic, no-one quite saw how. If your need is to know, not only with the warm wisdom of instinctive intelligence, but also with effective precision, you must first suffer the guillotine. Only after you have disentangled two strands of a single thread and laid them carefully side by side can you twist them together by your own act. The mind must have learnt to distinguish soma absolutely from psyche before it can be in a position to trace their interaction with the requisite finesse; and this applies not only to the human organism, but also to nature as a whole. It is the case that there is to be found in anthroposophy that immemorial understanding of tri-unity *in* man, in nature and in God, and *of* God and nature and man, which had long permeated the philosophy and religion of the East, before it continued to survive (often subterraneously) in the West in the doctrines of Platonism, Neo-Platonism, Hermetism, etc.; true that you will find it in Augustine, in pseudo-Dionysius, in Cusanus, in Bruno, in William Blake and a cloud of other witnesses, of whom Boehme is perhaps the outstanding representative. It would be surprising if it were not so. What differentiates anthroposophy from its "traditional" predecessors, both methodologically and in its content, is precisely its "post-revolutionary" status. It is, if you are that way minded, the perennial philosophy; but, if so, it is that philosophy risen again, and in a form determined by its having risen again, from the psychological and spiritual eclipse of the scientific revolution. To resume for a moment the metaphor I adopted at the outset of these remarks, it is because the two blood-relations were wise enough to separate for a spell as "family", that they are able to come together again in the new and more specifically human relationship of independence, fellowship and love.

Just how badly is it needed, a genuinely psychosomatic physiology? That is a question the reflective reader will answer for himself. For my own part, to select only one from a number of reasons that come to mind, I doubt whether any less deep-seated remedy will ultimately avail against a certain creeping-sickness now hardly less apparent from the *Times Literary Supplement* than in the Charing Cross Road; I mean the increasingly simian preoccupation of captive human fancy with the secretions and the excretions of its own physical body.

A few final words about the translation. I have varied slightly the order in which the Sections are arranged and in most cases have substituted my own titles for those in the original. The German word *Seele* feels to me to be much more at home in technical as well as non-technical contexts than the English *soul*; and this is still more so with the adjective *seelisch*, for which we have no equivalent except *soul-* (adjectival). It is not however somewhat aggressively technical, as *psyche* is. I have compromised by using *psyche* and *psychic* generally but by no means universally. Habits of speech alter fairly quickly in some areas of discourse. Coleridge apologised for *psychological* as an "insolens verbum". The same might possibly have been said of *psyche* in 1917, but hardly, I think, today and still less tomorrow. The mental or intelligential reference of *Geist* — operating towards exclusion, even from the sub-conscious imagination, of "physical qualities" — is more emphatic than that of *spirit*; and once again this is even truer of *Geistig* and *spiritual*. I doubt if much can be done about this; but I have sought to help a little by rather infrequently Englishing *Geistig* and *Geist-* (adjectival) as *noetic*. The distinctively English *mind* and *mental* sometimes appear to a translator of German as a sort of planets in the night sky of vocabulary and I have here and there adopted them both in *seelisch* and in *Geistig* contexts. And then of course there were those two thorns in the flesh of all who are rash enough to attempt translating philosophical or psychological German — *Vorstellung* and *vorstellen*. This is a problem that would bear discussing at some length. But it must suffice to say that I have mainly used *representation* and *represent* (after considering and rejecting *presentation* and *present*), occasionally substituting, where the context seemed to demand it, *idea* and *ideation*. The *very* meaning feels to me to lurk somewhere *between* the English terms — which is a good reason for using them both. Other usages are based on similar considerations and reflection. As to any habitual reader of Steiner who may suspect that I have taken too many liberties, I can only assure him that, as far as I know, I have at least had no other motive than a keen desire to do the fullest possible justice to thought-laden sentences written by an Austrian in 1917, but being read (as I hope) by an Anglo-Saxon in and after 1970.

I
ANTHROPOLOGY AND ANTHROPOSOPHY

IN MAX DESSOIR'S book, *From Beyond the Soul*[1] there is a brief section in which the systematic noetic investigation, or spiritual science, called "anthroposophical" and associated with my name, is stigmatised as scientifically untenable. Now it might well be argued that any dialogue between someone with the scientific outlook of Dessoir and an upholder of this anthroposophical method must be a waste of time. For the latter necessarily posits a field of purely noetic experience which the former categorically denies and relegates to the realm of fantasy. Apparently then one can speak of spiritual science and its findings only to someone who is antecedently convinced of the factuality of that field.

This would be true enough if the spokesman for anthroposophy had nothing to bring forward but his own inner personal experiences, and if he then simply set these up alongside the findings of a science based on sensory observation and the scientific elaboration thereof. You could then say: the professor of science, so defined, must refuse to regard the experiences of the spiritual researcher as realities; the latter can only expect to impress those who have already adopted his own standpoint.

And yet this conclusion depends on a misconception of what I mean by anthroposophy. It is quite true that

---
[1] See Introduction, p. 11.

anthroposophy relies on psychic apprehensions that are dependent neither on sense-impressions nor on scientific propositions based on these and these alone. It must be conceded therefore that *prima facie* the two types of apprehension are divided from one another by an unbridgable gulf. Nevertheless this turns out not to be the case. There *is* a common ground on which the two methodologies may properly encounter one another and on which debate is possible concerning the findings of both. It may be characterised as follows.

The spokesman for anthroposophy maintains, on the basis of apprehensions that are not merely his private and personal experiences, that the process of human cognition can be further developed after a certain fixed point, a point beyond which scientific research, relying solely on sensory observation and inference therefrom, refuses to go. To avoid a lot of tedious paraphrases I propose, in what follows, to designate the methodology based on sensory observation and its subsequent inferential elaboration by

---

[2] Although the "anthroposophy" which I present relies for its findings on a ground quite different from that adopted by Robert Zimmermann in his book *Anthroposophie* (1881), I have felt entitled to avail myself of the verbal distinction he makes between anthroposophy and anthropology. The content of Zimmermann's "anthroposophy" however is simply an abstract schema compounded of the received findings of anthropology. The intuitive cognition, on which anthroposophy, as I use the term, is based, lies for him outside the realm of scientific methodology. His anthroposophy is differentiated from anthropology solely by the incidence that the concepts derived by the former from the latter have undergone a kind of Herbartian processing before they reappear as the content of Zimmermann's own, purely intellectual, ideology.

the term "anthropology"; requesting the reader's indulgence for this abnormal usage. It will be employed throughout strictly with that reference. Anthroposophical research, then, reckons to begin from where anthropology leaves off.²

The spokesman for anthropology limits himself to the method of relating his experience of concepts of the understanding with his experience through the senses. The spokesman for anthroposophy realises the fact that these concepts are capable (irrespective of the circumstance that they are to be related to sense-impressions) of opening a life of their own within the psyche. Further, that by the unfolding of this energy they effect a development in the psyche itself. And he has learnt how the psyche, if it pays the requisite attention to this process, makes the discovery that organs of spirit are disclosing their presence there. (In employing the expression "organs of spirit" I adopt, and extend, the linguistic usage of Goethe, who referred to "spiritual eyes" and "spiritual ears" in expounding his philosophical position).³ These organs amount to formations in the psyche analogous to what the sense-organs are in the body. It goes without saying that they

---

³ An exposition in greater detail together with a justification of this conception of "organs of spirit" will be found in my book *Vom Menschenrätsel* (4th Edition) as well as in my writings on Goethe's philosophical outlook.

Editor's Note. And the English reader should compare Coleridge (*Biographia Literaria*, Chapter XII): "...all the organs of sense are framed for a corresponding world of sense; and we have it. All the organs of spirit are framed for a correspondent world of spirit: though the latter organs are not developed in all alike."

are to be understood as *exclusively* psychic. Any attempt to connect them with some kind of somatic formation must be ruled out as far as anthroposophy is concerned. Spiritual organs are to be conceived as never in any manner departing from the psychic and entering the texture of the somatic. Any such encroachment is, for anthroposophy, a pathological formation with which it will have nothing whatever to do. And the whole manner in which the development of these organs is conceived should be enough to satisfy a bona fide enquirer that, on the subject of illusions, visions, hallucinations and so forth, the ideas of anthroposophy are the same as those that are normally accepted in anthropology.[4] When the findings of anthroposophy are equated with abnormal experiences, miscalled "psychic", or "psychical", the argument is invariably based on misunderstanding or on an insufficient acquaintance with what anthroposophy actually maintains. Moreover no-one who had followed with a modicum of penetration the manner in which anthroposophy treats of the development of spiritual organs could possibly slip into the notion of its being a path that could lead to pathological syndromes. On the contrary, given such penetration, it will be realised that all the stages of psychic apprehension which a human being, according to anthroposophy, experiences in his progress towards intuition of spirit, lie in a domain exclusively

---

[4] The inner experiences, which the psyche has to undergo in order to be able to make use of its spiritual organs, are dealt with in a number of my writings and particularly in the book *Knowledge of the Higher Worlds* and the second part of *Occult Science: an Outline*.

psychic; so that sensory experience and normal intellectual activity continue alongside of them unaltered from what they were before this territory was opened up. The plethora of misunderstandings that are current upon this aspect of anthroposophical cognition arise from the fact that many people have difficulty in focusing their attention on what is purely and distinctively psychic. The power to form ideas fails them, unless it is supported by some surreptitious reference to sensory phenomena. Failing that, their mental capacity wilts, and ideation sinks to an energy-level below that of dreaming — to the level of dreamless sleep, where it is no longer conscious. It may be said that the consciousness of such minds is congested with the after-effects, or the actual effects, of sense-impressions; and this congestion entails a corresponding slumber of all that *would* be recognised as psychic, if it could be seized at all. It is even true to say that many minds approach the properly psychic with hopeless misunderstanding precisely because they are unable, when it confronts them, to stay awake, as they do when they are confronted by the sensory content of consciousness. Such is the predicament of all in whom the faculty of vigilant attention is only strong enough for the purposes of everyday life. This sounds surprising, but I would recommend anyone who finds it incredible to ponder carefully a certain objection raised by Brentano against the philosopher William James. "It is necessary," writes Brentano, "to distinguish between the act of sensing and that upon which the act is directed and the two are as certainly different from one another as my present recollection of a past event is from the event itself; or, to take an even more drastic example, as my hatred of an enemy is from the object of that hate." He adds that the error he is nailing does "turn up here and there", and he continues:

> Among others it has been embraced by William James, who endeavoured to establish it in a longish address to the International Congress on Psychology in 1905. Because, when I look into a room, there is evidently not only the room but also my looking; because fancied images of sensible objects only distinguish themselves gradually from objectively stimulated ones; because, finally, we call some bodies beautiful, and yet the difference between beautiful and ugly relates to different emotions — therefore we must stop regarding physical and psychic phenomena as two different classes of appearance! I find it hard to understand how the speaker himself could be unaware of the weakness of these arguments. To appear simultaneously is not to appear as one and the same. For simultaneity is less than identity. That was why Descartes could recommend his readers, without fear of contradiction, to deny, at least to begin with, that the room which I see *is*, and to hold fast to the-fact-that-I-see-it as the one thing free from doubt. But if the first argument falls to the ground, then obviously the second one does also. For why should it matter that fancy differs from seeing only by the degree of intensity, since, even if the degrees of intensity were the same total similarity between fancying and seeing could prove no more than the similarity of fancying to a psychic phenomenon? Finally there is the argument from beauty. Surely it is a very odd sort of logic which draws, from the fact that pleasure in the beautiful is something psychic, the

conclusion that that, with the appearance whereof the pleasure is connected, must *also* be something psychic! If that were so, every displeasure would be identical with what we are displeased about; and a man would have to be very careful not to regret a past mistake, because the regret (being identical with the mistake) would repeat the mistake itself.

For all these reasons there ought not to be much fear that the authority of James, which he unfortunately shares with that of Mach among German psychologists, will seduce many people into overlooking such a glaring distinction.

All the same, this "overlooking of glaring distinctions" is far from rare. The reason is that our faculty of ideation only operates vigilantly with the *somatic* component of representation, the sense-impressions; the concurrent psychic factor is present to consciousness only to the feeble extent of experiences had during sleep. The stream of experience comes to us in two currents: one of them is apprehended wakefully; the other, the psychic, is seized concurrently, but only with a degree of awareness similar to the mentality of sleep, that is, with virtually no awareness at all. It is impermissible to ignore the fact that, during ordinary waking life, the psychology of sleep does not simply leave off; it continues alongside our waking experience; so that the specifically psychic only enters the field of perception if the subject is awake not only to the sense world (as is the case with ordinary consciousness), but also to the existentially psychic — which is the case with *intuitive consciousness*. It makes very little difference whether this latter (the slumber that persists within the waking state) is simply denied on crudely materialistic grounds or whether, with James, it is lumped in with the physical organism. The results in either case are much the same. Both ways lead to ill-starred myopias. Yet we ought not to be surprised that the psychic so often remains unperceived, when even a philosopher like William James is incapable of distinguishing it properly from the physical.[5]

With those who are no better able than James to keep the positively psychic separate from the content of the psyche's experience through the senses, it is difficult to speak of that part of the soul wherein the development of spiritual organs is observable. Because this development occurs at the very point on which they are incapable of directing attention. And it is just this point that leads from intellectual to intuitive knowledge.[6]

It should be noted however that such a capacity to observe the authentically psychic is very elementary; it is the indispensable precondition, but it assures to the mind's eye no more than the bare possibility of looking whither anthroposophy looks to find the psychic organs. This first glimpse bears the same relation to a soul fully equipped with the spiritual organs of which anthroposophy speaks as an undifferentiated living cell does to a full-blown creature furnished with sense-organs.

---

[5] This quickening of psychic faculties which in ordinary life remain unawakened is dealt with in greater detail in my *Vom Menschenrätsel*.

[6] See also Section II: *The Philosophical Bearing of Anthroposophy*.

The soul is only conscious of possessing a particular organ of spirit to the extent that it is able to make use of it. For these organs are not something static; they are in continual movement. And when they are not being employed, it is not possible to be conscious of their presence. Thus, their apprehension and their use coincide. The manner in which their development and, with that, the possibility of observing them, is brought about will be found described in my anthroposophical writings. There is one point however I must briefly touch on here.

Anyone given to serious reflection on the experiences occasioned through sense phenomena keeps coming up against questions which that reflection itself is at first inadequate to answer. This leads to the establishment by those who represent anthropology of boundaries of cognition. Recall, for instance, Du Bois-Reymond's oration on the frontiers of natural knowledge, in which he maintained that man cannot know what is the actual nature of matter or of any elementary phenomenon of consciousness. All he can do is to come to a halt at these points in his reflection and acknowledge to himself: "there are boundaries of knowledge which the human mind cannot cross". After that there are two possible attitudes he may adopt. He may rest content with the fact that knowledge is only attainable inside this limited zone and that anything outside the fence is the province of feelings, hopes, wishes, inklings. Or he can make a new start and form hypotheses concerning an extra-sensory realm. In that case he is making use of the understanding, in the faith that its judgments can be carried into a realm of which the senses perceive nothing. But, in doing so, he puts himself in peril of the agnostic's objection: that the understanding is not entitled to form judgments concerning a reality for which it lacks the foundation of sense-perception. For it is these alone which could give content to judgments, and without such content concepts are empty.

The attitude of an anthroposophically oriented science of the spirit to boundaries of cognition resembles neither the one nor the other of these. Not the second, because it is in substantial agreement with the view that the mind must lose the whole ground for reflection, if it rests satisfied with such ideas as are acquired through the senses and yet seeks to apply these ideas beyond the province of the senses. Not the first, because it realises that contact with those "boundaries" of knowledge evokes a certain psychic experience that has nothing to do with the content of ideation won from the senses. Certainly, if it is only *this* content that the mind presents to itself, then it is obliged, on further introspection, to admit: "this content can disclose nothing for cognition except a reproduction of sensory experience". But it is otherwise if the mind goes a step further and asks itself: What is the nature of its own experience, when it fills itself with the kind of thoughts that are evoked by its contact with the normal boundaries of cognition? The same exercise of introspection may then lead it to say: "I cannot know in the ordinary sense with such thoughts: but if I succeed in inwardly contemplating this very impotence to know, I am made aware of how these thoughts become active in me". Considered as normally cognitive ideas they remain silent, but as their silence communicates itself more and more to a man's consciousness, they acquire an inner life of their own, which becomes one with the life of the soul. And then the soul notices that this experience has brought it to a pass that may be compared with that of a blind creature, which has not yet done much to cultivate its sense of touch. Initially, such a creature would simply keep on knocking up against things. It would sense the resistance of external realities. But out of this generalised sensation it could develop an inner life informed with a primitive consciousness — no longer a general sensation of collisions, but a consciousness that begins to diversify that sensation, remarking distinctions between hardness and softness, smoothness and roughness and so forth.

In the same way, the soul is able to undergo, and to diversify, the experience it has with ideas it forms at the boundaries of cognition and to learn from them that those boundaries are simply events that occur when the psyche is stimulated by a touch of the spiritual world. The moment of awareness of such boundaries turns into an experience comparable with tactile experience in the sense world.[7] In what it previously termed boundaries of cognition, it now sees a pneumato-psychic stimulus through a spiritual world. And out of the pondered experience it can have with the different boundaries of

---

[7] The boundaries of cognition referred to are not only those, comparatively few in number, of which there is general awareness. A great many are encountered along the avenues of self-reflection — which have to be explored on the way to immediate relation with reality. See also Section III: *Concerning the Limits of Knowledge*.

cognition, the general sense of a world of spirit separates out into a manifold perception thereof.

This is the manner in which the, so to say, humblest mode of perceptibility of the spiritual world becomes experiential. All that has been dealt with so far is the initial opening up of the psyche to the world of spirit, but it does show that anthroposophy, as I use the term, and the noetic experiences it ensues, do not connote all manner of nebulous personal affects, but a methodical development of authentic inner experience. This is not the place to demonstrate further how such inchoate spiritual perception is then improved by further psychic exercises and achievements, so that it becomes legitimate to use the vocabulary of touch in this context, or of other and "higher" modes of perception. For a conative psychology of this kind I must refer the reader to my anthroposophical books and articles. My present object is to state the *principle* basic to "spiritual perception" as it is understood in anthroposophy.

I shall offer one other analogy to illustrate how the whole psychology of anthroposophical spiritual investigation differs from that of anthropology. Look at a few grains of wheat. They can be applied for the purposes of nutrition. Alternatively they can be planted in the soil, so that other wheat plants develop from them. The representations and ideas acquired through sensory experience can be retained in the mind with the effect that what is experienced in them is a reproduction of sensory reality. And they can also be experienced in another way: the energy they evince in the psyche by virtue of what they *are*, quite apart from the fact that they reproduce phenomena, can be allowed to act itself out. The first way may be compared with what happens to wheat grains when they are assimilated by a living creature as its means of nourishment. The second with the engendering of a new wheat plant through each grain. Of course we must bear in mind that, in the analogy, what is brought forth is a plant similar to the parent plant; whereas from an idea active in the mind the outcome is a force available for the formation of organs of the spirit. It must also be borne in mind that initial awareness of such inner forces can only be kindled by particularly potent ideas, like those "frontiers of knowledge" of which we have been speaking; but when once the mind has been alerted to the presence of such forces, other ideas and representations may also serve, though not quite so well, for further progress in the direction it has now taken.

The analogy illustrates something else that anthroposophical research discovers concerning the actual psychology of mental representation. It is this. Whenever a seed of corn is processed for the purposes of nutrition, it is lifted out of the developmental pattern which is proper to it, and which ends in the formation of a new plant, but so also is a representation, whenever it is applied by the mind in producing a mental copy of sense-perception, diverted from its proper teleological pattern. The corresponding further development proper to a representation is to function as a force in the development of the psyche. Just as little as we find the laws of development built in to a plant, if we examine it for its nutritive value, do we find the essential nature of an idea or a representation, when we investigate its adequacy in reproducing for cognition the reality it mediates. That is not to say that no such investigation should be undertaken. It can all be investigated just as much as can the nutritive value of a seed. But then, just as the latter enquiry throws light on something quite different from the developmental laws of plant growth, so does an epistemology, which tests representations by the criterion of their value as images for cognition, reach conclusions about something other than the essential nature of ideation. The seed, as such, gave little indication of turning into nourishment: nor does it lie with representations, as such, to deliver copies for cognition. In fact, just as its application as nutriment is something quite external to the seed itself, so is cognitive reproduction irrelevant for representation. The truth is that what the psyche does lay hold of in its representations is its own waxing existence. Only through its own activity does it come about that the representations turn into media for the cognition of some reality.[8]

There remains the question: how *do* representations turn into media for cognition? Anthroposophical observation, availing itself as it does of spiritual organs, inevitably answers this question differently from epistemological theories that renounce them. Its answer is as follows.

---

[8] All this is dealt with at greater length in the final section of Vol. 2 of my *Die Rätsel der Philosophie*, under the heading: "Sketch Plan for an Anthroposophy".

Representations strictly as such — considered as what they themselves originally *are* — do indeed form part of the *life* of the soul; but they cannot become *conscious* there as long as the soul does not consciously use its spiritual organs. So long as they retain their original vitality they remain unconscious. The soul *lives* by means of them, but it can *know* nothing *of* them. They have to suppress (*herabdämpfen*) their own life in order to become conscious experiences of normal consciousness. This suppression is effected by every sense perception. Consequently, when the mind receives a sense impression, there is a benumbing (*Herablähmung*) of the life of the representation, and it is this benumbed representation which the psyche experiences as the medium of a cognition of outer reality.[9] All the representations and ideas that are related by the mind to an outer sense reality are inner spiritual experiences, whose life has been suppressed. In all our thoughts about an outer world of the senses, we have to do with deadened representations. And yet the *life* of the representation is not just annihilated; rather it is disjoined from the area of consciousness but continues to subsist in the nonconscious provinces of the psyche. That is where it is found again by the organs of the spirit. Just as the deadened ideas of the soul can be related to the sense world, so can the living ideas apprehended by spiritual organs be related to the spiritual world. But "boundary" concepts of the kind spoken of above, by their very nature,

---

[9] See also Section IV: *Concerning Abstraction*.

refuse to be deadened. Consequently they resist being related to any sense reality. And for that reason they become points of departure for spiritual perception.

In my anthroposophical writings I have applied the term "imaginal" to representations that are apprehended by the psyche as living. It is a misunderstanding to confound the reference of this word with the *form* of expression (imagery) which has to be employed in order to analogously *suggest* such representations. What the word does mean may be elucidated in the following manner. If someone has a sense-perception while the outer object is impressing him, then the perception has a certain inner potency for him. If he turns away from the object, then he can re-present it to himself in a purely internal representation. But the intrinsic strength of the representation has now been reduced. Compared with the representation effected in the presence of the object, it is more or less shadowy. If he wants to enliven these shadowy representations of ordinary consciousness, he impregnates them with echoes of actual contemplation. He converts the representation into a visual *image*. Now such images are no other than the joint effects of representation and sensory life combined. But the "imaginal" representations of anthroposophy are not effected in this way at all. In order to bring them to pass, the soul must be familiar with the inner *process* that combines psychic representation with sense-impression, so familiar that it can hold at arm's length the influx of the sense-impressions themselves (or of their echoes in after-experience) into the act of representing. This keeping at bay of post-sense-experiences can only be achieved, if the man has detected the way in which the *activity* of representing is pre-empted by these after-experiences. Not until then is he in a position to combine his spiritual organs with the act itself and thereby to receive impressions of spiritual reality.

Thus the act of representing is impregnated from quite another side than in the case of sense-perception. And thus the mental experiences are positively different from those evoked by sense-perception. And yet they are not beyond all possibility of expression. They may be expressed by the following means. When a man perceives the colour *yellow*, he has an experience that is not simply optical but is also affective and empathetic, an experience of the nature of feeling. It may be more or less pronounced in different human beings, but it is never wholly absent. There is a beautiful chapter in Goethe's *Farbenlehre* on the "sensuous-moral effect of colours", in which he has described with great penetration the emotional by-effects for red, yellow, green and so forth. Now when the mind perceives something from a particular province of the spirit, it may happen that this spiritual perception has the same emotional by-effect as the sensory perception of yellow. The man knows that he is having this or that spiritual experience; and what he has before him in the representation is of course not *the same* as in a representation of the colour yellow. But he does have, as emotional by-effect, the same inner experience as when the colour yellow is before his eyes. He may then aver that he perceives the spirit experience as "yellow". Of course he could choose to be more precise, always being careful to say: "the mind apprehends somewhat that affects the soul rather as the colour yellow affects it". But such elaborate verbal precautions ought to be unnecessary for anyone who is already acquainted through anthroposophical literature with the process leading to spiritual perception. This literature gives a clear enough warning that the reality open to spiritual perception does *not* confront the organ of spirit after the fashion of an attenuated sense-object or event, nor in such a way that it could be rendered in ideas that are intuitions of sense (*sinnlich-anschauliche*) as commonly understood.[10]

*   *   *

Just as the mind becomes acquainted through its spiritual organs with the spiritual world outside of a man, so does it come to know the spirit-being of the man himself. Anthroposophy observes this spirit-being as a member of the spiritual world. It proceeds from observation of a part of the spiritual world to ideas of human being which represent to it the spiritual man as he reveals himself in the human body. Anthropology, too, coming from the opposite direction, proceeds to ideas of human being. Once anthroposophy has reached the stage of developing the methods of observation already described, it attains to intuitions concerning the spiritual

---

[10] See also Section V: *Concerning the Nature of Spiritual Perception.*

core of the human being as that reveals itself, within the sense-world, in the body. The acme of this self-revelation is the consciousness that permits sense-impressions to persist in the form of representations. Proceeding, as it does, *from* experiences of the extra-human spiritual world *to* the human being, anthroposophy finds the latter subsisting in a sensuous body and, within that body, developing the consciousness of sensible reality. The last thing it reaches is the soul's activity in representation which is expressible in coherent imagery. Thereafter, and at the end, so to speak, of its journey of spiritual investigation, it can extend its gaze further; it can observe how positive activity in representation becomes half-paralysed through the percipient senses. It is this deadened representation process that anthroposophy sees (illumined from the spirit-side) as characterising the life of man in the sense-world, in so far as he is a representing being. Its philosophy of man is the final outcome of prior researches conducted purely in the realm of the spirit. Through what has transpired in the course of those researches, it comes at its notion of the human being living in the sense-world.

Anthropology investigates the kingdoms of the sense-world. It also arrives, in due course, at the human being. It sees him combining the facts of the sense-world in his physical organism in such a way that consciousness arises, and that through consciousness outer reality is given in representations. The anthropologist sees these representations as arising out of the human organism. And at that point, observing in that way, he is more or less brought to a halt. He cannot, *via* anthropology alone, apprehend any inner structural laws in the act of ideation or representation. Anthroposophy, at the end of the journey that has taken its course in spiritual experiencing, continues contemplating the spiritual core of man so far as that manifests itself through the perceptions of the senses. Similarly anthropology, at the end of the journey that has taken its course in the province of the senses, can only continue endeavouring to contemplate the way in which sensuous man acts on his sense-perceptions. In doing so, it discovers that this operation is sustained, not by the laws of somatic life, but by the mental laws of logic. But logic is not a region that can be explored in the same fashion as the other regions of anthropological enquiry. Logically ordered thought is answerable to laws that can no longer be termed those of the physical organism. Inasmuch as a man is operating with them, what becomes apparent is the same being whom anthroposophy has encountered at the end of *its* journey. Only, the anthropologist sees this being after the fashion in which it is illumined from the sense side. He sees the deadened representations, the ideas; he also concedes, in acknowledging the validity of logic, that the laws governing those ideas belong to a world, which interlocks with the sense-world, but is not identical with it. In the process of ideation carried on by a logical being, anthropology discovers sensuous man projecting into the spiritual world. By this route it arrives at a philosophy of man as a final outcome of its investigations. Everything that has led up to it is to be found purely in the realm of the senses.[11]

Rightly pursued, therefore, the two approaches, anthroposophical and anthropological, converge and meet in one point. Anthroposophy contributes the image of the living human spirit, showing how, through sense existence, this develops the consciousness that obtains between birth and death, while at the same time its supersensible consciousness is deadened. Anthropology contributes the image of sensuous man, apprehending in the moment of consciousness his selfhood but towering into a subsistence in the spirit that extends beyond birth and death. In this coincidence a genuinely fruitful understanding between anthroposophy and anthropology is possible. It cannot fail, if both disciplines terminate in philosophy and humanity. Certainly the philosophy of humanity which stems from anthroposophy will furnish an image of man delineated by methods quite other than those of the image furnished by the humanist philosophy stemming from anthropology. Yet close observers of the one image and of the other will find that their ideas accord, as the negative plate of a competent photographer accords with his positive print.

These observations began by posing the question whether fruitful dialogue is possible between anthropology and anthroposophy. They have perhaps succeeded in showing that the answer, at least from the anthroposophical point of view, is in the affirmative.

---

[11] Compare Section II.

II
THE PHILOSOPHICAL BEARING OF ANTHROPOSOPHY

NO-ONE, WHO AIMS at achieving a radical relation between his own thought and contemporary philosophical ideas, can avoid the issue, raised in the first paragraph of this book, of the existential status of the psyche. This he will have to justify not only to himself, but also in the light of those ideas. Now many people do not feel this need, since they are acquainted with the authentically psychic through immediate inner experience (*Erleben*) and know how to distinguish that from the psychic apprehension (*Erfahren*) effected through the senses. It strikes them as an unnecessary, perhaps an irritating, intellectual hair-splitting. And if *they* are positively averse, the more philosophically minded are often unwilling for a different reason. They are unwilling to concede to inner soul experiences any other status than that of subjective apprehensions without cognitive significance. They are little disposed therefore to ransack their philosophical concepts for those elements in them that could lead on to anthroposophical ideas. These repugnances, coming from opposite sides, make the exposition extraordinarily difficult. But it is necessary. For in our time the only kind of ideas to which cognitive validity can be assigned are such as will bear the same kind of critical examination as the laws of natural science must satisfy, before they can claim to have been established.

To establish, epistemologically, the validity of anthroposophical ideas, it is first of all necessary to conceive as precisely as possible the manner in which they are experienced. This can be done in several very different ways. Let us attempt to describe two of them. The first way requires that we observe the phenomenon of memory. Rather a weak point incidentally in current philosophical theory; for the concepts we find there concerning memory throw very little light on it. I take my departure from ideas which I have, in point of fact, reached by anthroposophical methods, but which can be fully supported both philosophically and physiologically. Limitations of space will not permit of my making good this assertion in the present work. I hope to do so in a future one.[1] I am convinced, however, that anyone who succeeds in candidly surveying the findings of modern physiological and psychological science will find that they support the following observations.

Representations stimulated by sense-impressions enter the field of unconscious human experience. From there they can be brought up again, remembered. Representations themselves are a purely psychic reality; but *awareness* of them in normal waking life is somatically conditioned. Moreover the psyche, bound up as it is with the body, cannot by using its own forces raise representations from their unconscious to their conscious condition. For that it requires the forces of the body. To the end of normal memory the body has to function, just as the body has to function in the processes of its sense-

---

[1] I have not been able to trace where, if at all, this intention was carried out – *Editor*.

organs, in order to bring about representations through the senses. If I am to represent a sensory event, a somatic activity must first come about within the sense organs; and, within the psyche, the representation appears as its result. In the same way, if I am to *remember* a representation or idea, an inner somatic activity (in refined organs), an activity polarically counter to the activity of the senses, must occur; and, as a result, the remembered representation comes forth. This representation is related to a sensory event which was presented to my soul at some time in the past. I represent that event to myself through an inner experience, to which my somatic organisation enables me.

Keep clearly in mind the character of such a memory-presentation, and with its help you approach the character of anthroposophical ideas. They are certainly not memory-presentations, but they issue in the psyche in a similar way. Many people, anxious to form ideas about the spiritual world in a less subtle way, find this disappointing. But the spiritual world cannot be experienced any more solidly than a happening in the sense-world apprehended in the past but no longer present to the sight. In the case of memory we have seen that our ability to remember such a happening comes from the energy of the somatic organisation. To the experience of the existentially psychic, on the other hand, as distinct from that of memory, this energy can make no contribution. Instead, the soul must awaken in itself the ability to accomplish with certain representations what the body accomplishes with the representations of the senses, when it implements their recall. The former — elicited from the depths of the psyche solely through the energy of the psyche, as memory-presentations are elicited from the depths of human nature through its somatic organisation — are representations related to the spiritual world. They are available to every soul. What has to be won, in order to become aware of them, is the energy to elicit them from the depths of the psyche by a purely psychic activity. As the remembered representations of the senses are related to a past sense-impression, so are these others related to a nexus between the psyche and the domain of spirit, a nexus which is not *via* the sense-world. The human soul stands towards the spiritual world, as the whole human being stands towards a forgotten actuality. It comes to the knowledge of that world, if it brings, to the point where they awake, energies which are similar to those bodily forces that promote memory. Thus, ideas of the authentically psychic depend for their philosophical validation on the kind of inquiry into the life within us that leads us to find there an activity purely psychic, which yet resembles in some ways the activity exerted in remembering.

A second way of forming a concept of the purely psychic is as follows. The attention may be directed to what anthropological observation has to say about the willing (operant) human being. An impulse of will that is to be carried into effect has as its ground the mental representation of what is to be willed. The dependence of this representation on the bodily organisation (nervous system) can be physiologically discerned. Bound up with the representation there is a nuance of feeling, an affective sympathy with the represented, which is the reason why this representation furnishes the impulse for a willed act. But from that point on psychic experience disappears into the depths; and the first thing that reappears in consciousness is the result. What is next represented, in fact, is the movement we make in order to achieve the represented goal. (Theodor Ziehen puts all this very clearly in his physiological psychology.) We can now perhaps see how, in the case of a willed act, the conscious process of mental representation is suspended in regard to the central moment of willing itself. That which is psychically experienced in the willing of an operation executed through the body, does not penetrate normal consciousness. But we do see plainly enough that that willing is realised through an *act* of the body. What is much harder to see is, that the psyche, when it is observing the laws of logic and seeking the truth by connecting ideas together, is *also* unfolding will. A will which is not to be circumscribed within physiological laws. For, if that were so, it would be impossible to distinguish an illogical — or simply an a-logical — chain of ideas from one which follows the laws of logic. (Superficial chatter around the fancy that logical consequence could be a property the mind acquires through adapting itself to the outer world, need not be taken seriously.) In this willing, which takes place entirely within the psyche, and which leads to logically grounded convictions, we can detect the permeation of the soul by an entirely spiritual activity.

Of what goes on in the will, when it is directed outwards, ordinary ideation knows as little as a man knows of himself when he is asleep. Something similar is true of his being regulated by logic in the formation of his convictions; he is less fully conscious of this than he is of the actual content of such convictions. Nevertheless anyone capable of looking inward, albeit only in the anthropological mode, will be able to form a concept of the co-presence of this being-regulated-by logic to normal consciousness. He will come to realise that the human being knows of this being-regulated, in the manner that he knows while *dreaming*. It is paradoxical but perfectly correct to say: normal consciousness knows the content of its convictions; but it only dreams of the regulation by logic that is extant in the pursuit of these convictions. Thus we see that, in ordinary-level consciousness, the human being *sleeps* through his willing, when he unfolds and exercises his will in an outward direction; he *dreams* his willing, when, in his thinking, he is seeking for convictions. Only it is clear that, in the latter instance, what he dreams of cannot be anything corporeal, for otherwise logical and physiological laws would coincide. The concept to be grasped is that of the willing that lives in the mental pursuit of truth. That is also the concept of an existentially psychic.

From both of these epistemological approaches, in the sense of anthroposophy, to the concept of the existentially psychic (and they are not the only possible ones), it becomes evident how sharply this concept is divorced from visions, hallucinations, mediumship or any kind of abnormal psychic activity. For the origin of all these abnormalities must be sought in the physiologically determinable. But the psychic, as anthroposophy understands it, is not only something that is experienced in the mode of normal and healthy consciousness; it is something that is experienced, even while representations are being formed, in total vigilance — and is experienced *in the same way* that we remember a happening undergone earlier in life, or alternatively in the same way that we experience the logically conditioned formation of our convictions. It will be seen that the cognitive experience of anthroposophy proceeds by way of representations and ideas that maintain the character of that normal consciousness with which, as well as with reality, the external world endows us; while at the same time they add to it endowments leading into the domain of the spirit. By contrast the visionary, hallucinatory, etc. type of experience subsists in a consciousness that adds nothing to the norm, but actually takes away from it by eliminating some faculties already acquired; so that there the level of consciousness falls below the level that obtains in conscious sense-perception.

For those of my readers who are acquainted with what I have written elsewhere[2] concerning recollection and memory I would add the following. Representations that have entered the unconscious and are subsequently remembered are to be located, so long as they remain unconscious, as representations within that component of the human body which is there identified as a life-body

---

[2] For example, in *Occult Science: an Outline*, pp. 45-8 and 336.

(etheric body). But the *activity*, through which representations anchored in the life-body are remembered, belongs to the physical body. I emphasise this in case some, who jump hastily to conclusions, should construe as an inconsistency what is in fact a distinction made necessary by this particular context.

III
CONCERNING THE LIMITS OF KNOWLEDGE

THE INNER NATURE of man demands that he experience his relation with ultimate reality. Among thinkers who pursue this goal with untiring energy we find a large number discoursing on certain "boundaries" of knowledge. And, if we listen attentively, we cannot help noticing how collision with these boundaries, when it is experienced by a candid mind, tends in the direction of an inner psychic apprehension, a "purely noetic experience" such as was indicated in the first paragraph of this book. Consider how the profoundly able mind of Friedrich Theodor Vischer, in the packed essay he wrote on Johannes Volkelt's book *Dream-Phantasy* (*Traumphantasie*), reports its own reaction to one such limit of cognition:

> "No mind where no nerve-centre, where no brain", say our opponents. No nerve-centre, *we* say, no brain unless it had been first prepared for by innumerable stages from below upwards. It is easy to babble, with a sneer, about Mind careering through granite and chalk — just as easy as it is for us to ask, with a sneer, how the albumen in the brain flies up aloft into ideas. Human knowledge is extinguished at any attempt to span the distance from one step to the other.
> It will remain a secret how it comes about that nature — beneath which spirit must somehow or other be slumbering — presents itself as such a backlash of spirit that we bruise ourselves on it. The diremption appears so absolute that Hegel's formulation of it as "Being other" and "Being outside itself", brilliant as it is, says almost nothing; it

simply drapes the abruptness of the party wall. We may look to Fichte for a really adequate acknowledgment of the abruption and of the shock of the backlash, but we still find no explanation of it. (Compare F. T. Vischer: "Old and New" [*Altes und Neues*], 1881, Part I, p. 229 f.)

Vischer lays his finger on the kind of issue with which anthroposophy too engages. But he fails to realise that, precisely at such a frontier of knowledge as this, another mode of knowledge can begin. He desires to go on living on these frontiers with the same brand of cognition that sufficed *until he reached them*. Anthroposophy seeks to demonstrate that the possibility of systematic knowledge (science) does not cease at the point where ordinary cognition "bruises" itself, at the point where this "abruption" and these "shocks" from the backlash make themselves felt; but that, on the contrary, the experiences that ensue from them lead naturally towards the development of another type of cognition, which transforms the backlash into perception of spirit — a perception which at the outset, in its initial stage, may be compared with *tactile* perception in the realm of the senses.

In Part III of *Altes und Neues* Vischer says: "Very well: there is no soul alongside of the body (he means, for the materialists); what we call matter simply becomes soul at the highest level of organisation known to us, in the brain; and soul evolves to mind or spirit. In other words, we are to be satisfied with a half-baked concept, which for the divisive understanding is a simple contradiction." Anthroposophy echoes and supplements this with: Very well: for the divisive understanding there *is* a contradiction. But for the soul, the contradiction becomes the point of departure of a knowledge before which the divisive understanding is pulled up short, because it encounters the backlash of actual spirit.

Again, Gideon Spicker, the author of a series of discerning publications, who also wrote *Philosophical Confession of a Former Capuchin* (*Philosophische Bekenntnis eines ehemaligen Kapuziners*, 1910) identifies incisively enough one of the confining limits of ordinary cognition:

> Whatever philosophy a man confesses, whether it is dogmatic or sceptical, empirical or transcendental, critical or eclectic, every one, without exception, starts from an unproven and unprovable premise, namely the *necessity of thinking*. No investigation ever gets behind this necessity, however deep it may dig. It has to be simply, and groundlessly, accepted; every attempt to prove its validity already presupposes it. Beneath it yawns a bottomless abyss, a ghastly darkness, illuminated by no ray of light. We know not whence that necessity comes, nor whither it leads. As to whether a gracious God or whether an evil demon implanted it in the reason, we are equally uncertain. (p. 30)

Reflection on the nature of thought, then, leads of itself to one of the frontiers of normal cognition. Anthroposophy occupies this frontier; it knows how necessity confronts and blocks discursive thought like an impenetrable wall. But when the *act* of thinking is *experienced* as such, the wall becomes penetrable. This *experienced* thinking finds a light of contemplation wherewith to illuminate the "darkness illuminated by no ray of light" of merely discursive thought. It is only for the dominion of the senses that the abyss is bottomless; if we do not halt before it, but make up our minds to risk going ahead with thought, beyond the point at which it has to jettison all that the senses have furnished to it, then in that "bottomless abyss" we find the realities of the spirit.

One could continue almost indefinitely exemplifying the reaction of serious minds before the "frontiers of knowledge". And it would serve to show that anthroposophy has its proper place as the inevitable product of mental evolution in the modern age. There are plenty of prophetic signs, if we know how to read them.

IV
CONCERNING ABSTRACTION

ON PAGE 29 the expression "benumbing" (*Herablähmung*) is used of representations as they turn into imitations of sensory reality. It is in this "benumbing" that we must locate the positive event that underlies the phase of abstraction in the process of cognition. The mind forms *concepts* of sensory reality. For any theory of knowledge the question is how that, which it retains within itself as concept of a real being or event, is related to such real being or event. Has the somewhat that I carry around in me as the concept of a wolf any relation at all to a particular reality, or is it simply a schema that I have constructed for myself by withdrawing my attention (abstracting) from anything peculiar to this wolf or that wolf, and to which nothing in the real world corresponds? This question received extensive treatment in the medieval conflict between Nominalism and Realism: for the Nominalists nothing about the world is real except the visible materials extant in it as a single individual, flesh, blood, bones and so forth. The concept "wolf" is "merely" a conceptual aggregate of the properties common to different wolves. To this the Realist objects: any material found in an individual wolf is also to be found in other animals. There must then be something that disposes the materials into the living coherence they exhibit in the wolf. This constituent reality is given by way of the concept. It cannot be denied that Vincent Knauer, the distinguished specialist in Aristotelian and medieval philosophy, has something, when he says in his book, *Fundamental Problems of Philosophy* (*Die Hauptprobleme der Philosophie*, Vienna, 1892):

> A wolf, for instance, consists of no different material constituents than a lamb; its material corporeality is composed of assimilated lambsflesh; yet the wolf does not become a lamb even if it eats nothing but lambs all its life. Whatever it is that makes it wolf, therefore, must obviously be something other than the "hyle", the sensory material, and that something, moreover, cannot possibly be a mere "thought-thing" even though it is accessible to thought alone, and not to the senses. It must be something active, therefore actual, therefore eminently real.

How after all does one get round this objection on a strictly anthropological view of what constitutes reality? It is not what is transmitted through the senses that produces the concept "wolf". On the other hand that concept, as present in ordinary-level consciousness, is certainly nothing *effective*. Merely by the energy of that concept the conformation of the "sensory" materials contained in a wolf could certainly not be brought about. The fact is that, with this question, anthropology comes up against one of its frontiers of knowledge. Anthroposophy demonstrates that, besides the relation of man to wolf, which is there in the sensory field, there is another relation as well. This latter does not, in its immediate specificity, reach into ordinary-level consciousness. But it does subsist as a *living* continuity between the human mind and the sensuously observed object. The vitality that subsists in the mind by virtue of this continuity is by the systematic understanding subdued, or benumbed, to a "concept". An abstract idea is a reality defunct, to enable its representation in ordinary-level consciousness, a reality in which the human being does in fact live in the process of sense-perception, but which does not become a conscious part of his life. The abstractness of ideas is brought about by an inner necessity of the psyche. Reality furnishes man with a living content. Of this living content he puts to death that part which invades his ordinary consciousness. He does so because he could not achieve self-consciousness as against the outer world if he were compelled to experience, in all its vital flux, his continuity *with* that world. Without the paralysing of this vital flow, the human being could only know himself as a scion comprised within a unity extending beyond the limits of his humanity; he would be an organ of a larger organism.

The manner in which the mind suffers its cognitive process to peter out into the abstractness of concepts is *not* determined by a reality external to itself. It is determined by the laws of development of man's own existence, which laws demand that, in the process of perception, he subdue his vital continuity with the outer world down to those abstract concepts that are the foundation whereon his self-consciousness grows and increases. That this is the case becomes evident to the mind, once it has developed its organs of spirit. By this means that living continuity with a spiritual reality lying outside the individual, which was referred to on pp. 32/33, is reconstituted. But, unless *self-consciousness* had been purchased in the first place from *ordinary-level* consciousness, it could not be amplified to intuitive consciousness. It follows that a healthy ordinary-level consciousness is a *sine qua non* of intuitive consciousness. Anyone who supposes that he can develop an intuitive consciousness without a healthy and active ordinary-level consciousness is making a very great mistake. On the contrary, normal and everyday consciousness has to accompany an intuitive consciousness at every single moment. Otherwise self-consciousness will be impaired and disorder introduced into the mind's relation to reality. It is to this kind of consciousness alone that anthroposophy looks for intuitive cognition; not to any sedating of ordinary-level consciousness.

V
CONCERNING THE NATURE OF SPIRITUAL PERCEPTION

PERCEPTIONS IN THE field of noetic reality do not persist within the psyche in the same way as do representations gained through sense-perception. While it is true that such perceptions may be usefully compared with the ideas of memory, on the lines indicated in Section II, their station within the psyche is nevertheless not the same as that of its memories. This is because what is experienced as spiritual perception cannot be preserved there in its immediate form. If a man wishes to have the same noetic perception over again, he must occasion it *anew* within the psyche. In other words the psyche's relation to the corresponding noetic reality must be deliberately re-established. And this renewal is not to be compared with the remembering of a sense-impression, but solely with the bringing into view once more of the same sense object as was there on the occasion of the former impression.

What *can*, within the memory, be retained of an actual spiritual perception is not the perception itself but the disposition of soul through which one attained to that perception. If my object is to repeat a spiritual perception which I had some while back, it is no use my trying to remember it. What I *should* try to remember is something that will call back the psychic preparations that led me to the perception in the first place. Perception then occurs through a process that does not depend on me.

It is important to be very conscious of this dual nature of the whole proceeding, because it is only in that way that one gains authentic knowledge of what is in fact *objective spirit*. Thereafter, it is true, the duality is modified for practical purposes, through the circumstance that the *content* of the spiritual perception can be carried over from the intuitive into ordinary-level consciousness. Then, within the latter, it becomes an abstract idea. And *this* can be later recollected in the ordinary manner. Nevertheless, in order to acquire a reliable psychic relation to the spiritual world, it is a very great advantage to cultivate assiduously the knowledge of three rather subtly differentiated mental processes: 1, psychic, or soul, processes leading up to a spiritual perception; 2, spiritual perceptions themselves; 3, spiritual perceptions translated into the concepts of ordinary consciousness.

VI
REPLY TO A FAVOURITE OBJECTION

THERE IS ONE objection often brought against anthroposophy, which is no less understandable than it is impermissible; understandable against the psychological background of those who advance it and impermissible because it traverses the whole spirit of anthroposophical research. I find it quite trivial, because the answer to it is readily available to anyone who follows with genuine understanding the literature written from the anthroposophical point of view. Only because it is always cropping up again do I repeat here some of the observations I added in 1914 to the sixth edition of my book *Theosophy*. It ought to be possible (so runs the objection) for the alleged findings of anthroposophical observation to be "proved" by strictly scientific, that is experimental, methods. The idea is that a few people, who maintain that they can achieve such results, should be confronted with a number of other people under strictly controlled experimental conditions, whereupon the "spiritual researchers" would be asked to declare what they have "seen" in the examining persons. For the experiment to succeed, their findings would have to coincide or at all events to share a high enough percentage of similarity to each other. It is, perhaps, not surprising that someone whose knowledge of anthroposophy does not include having understood it should keep on making demands of this kind. Their satisfaction would save him the trouble of working his way through to the *actual* proof, which consists in acquiring, as it is open to everyone to do, the ability to see for himself. But anyone who has really understood anthroposophy will have sufficient insight to realise that an experiment engineered on these lines is about as apt a way of getting results through genuinely spiritual intuition as stopping the clock is of telling the time. The preliminaries leading up to the conditions under which spiritual observation is possible have to be furnished by the psyche itself and by the total disposition of the psyche. External arrangements of the kind that lead to a natural-scientific experiment are not so furnished. For instance, one part of that same disposition must of necessity be, that the will-impulse prompting to an observation is *exclusively and without reservation* the original impulse of the person to make the observation. And that there should not be anything in the artificial external preparations that exerts a transforming influence upon that innermost impulse. At the same time — and it is surprising how this is nearly always overlooked — given these psychological conditions, everyone can procure the proofs for anthroposophy for himself; so that the "proofs" are in fact universally accessible. It will of course be indignantly denied; but the only real reason for insisting on "external proofs" is the fact that they can be obtained in reasonable comfort; whereas the authentically spiritual-scientific method is a laborious and disconcerting one.

What Brentano wanted was something very different from this demand for comfortable experimental verification of anthroposophical truths. He wanted to be able to work in a psychological laboratory. His longing for this facility frequently crops up in his writings, and he made repeated efforts to bring it about. The tragic intervention of circumstance obliged him to abandon the idea. Just because of his attitude to psychological questions he would have produced, with the help of such a laboratory, results of great importance. If the object is to establish the *best* conditions for obtaining results in the field of anthropological psychology (which extends just as far as those "boundaries of knowledge", where anthropology and anthroposophy encounter one another), then the answer is the kind of psychological laboratory Brentano envisaged. In such a laboratory there would be no need to hunt for ways of inducing manifestations of "intuitive consciousness" experimentally. The experimental techniques employed there would soon show how human nature is adapted for that kind of "seeing" and how the intuitive is entailed by the normal consciousness. Everyone who holds the anthroposophical point of view longs, as Brentano did, to be able to work in a genuine psychological laboratory; but for the present such a possibility is ruled out by the prejudices against anthroposophy that still prevail.

VII
PRINCIPLES OF PSYCHOSOMATIC PHYSIOLOGY[1]

MY OBJECT HERE is to present in outline certain conclusions I have reached concerning the relations between the psychic and the physical components of the human being. I may add that, in doing so, I place on record the results of a systematic spiritual investigation extending over a period of thirty years. It is only in the last few of those years that it has become practicable to formulate these results in concepts capable of verbal expression, and thus to bring the investigation to at least a temporary close. I must emphasise that it is the results and the results alone that I shall be presenting, or rather indicating, in what follows. Their foundation in fact can certainly be established on the basis of contemporary science. But to do this would require a substantial volume; and that my present circumstances do not permit of my writing.

If we are seeking for the actual relation between psychic and physical, it will not do to take as our starting-point Brentano's distribution of psychic experience into representation, judgment and the responses of love and hate. Partitioning in this way, we are led to shelve so many relevant considerations that we shall reach no reliable results. On the contrary we have to *start* from that very trichotomy of representation, feeling and will which Brentano rejected. If we survey the psychic experience of representation as a whole, and seek for the bodily

---
[1] See Introduction, pp. 13-15.

processes with which that experience is related, we shall find the appropriate nexus by relying substantially on the findings of current physiological psychology. The somatic correlatives to the psychic element in representation are observable in the processes of the nervous system, extending into the sense organs in one direction and into the interior physical organism in the other. Here, however wide the divergence in many respects between the anthroposophical point of view and that of contemporary science, that very science provides an excellent foundation.

It is otherwise when we seek to determine the somatic correlatives for feeling and willing. There we have first to blaze the requisite trail through the findings of current physiology. And once we have succeeded in doing so, we shall find that, just as representation is necessarily related to nervous activity, so feeling must be seen as related to that vital rhythm which is centred in, and connected with, the respiratory system; bearing in mind that, for this purpose, the rhythm of breathing must be traced right into the outermost peripheral regions of the organism. To arrive at concrete results here, the findings of physiological research need to be pursued in a direction which is as yet decidedly unfamiliar. If we take the trouble to do this, preliminary objections to bracketing feeling with respiration, all disappear, and what at first looks like an objection turns out to be a proof. Take one simple example from the wide range available: musical experience is dependent on some feeling, but the content of musical form subsists in representations furnished by auditory perception. How does musical emotion arise? The *representation* of the tonal shape (which depends on organ of hearing and neural process) is not yet the actual musical experience. That arises in the measure that the rhythm of breathing, continuing further into the brain, confronts within that organ the effects produced there by ear and nervous system. The psyche now lives, not alone in what is heard and represented, or thought, but in the breathing rhythm. Something is released in the breathing rhythm through the fact that neural process impinges on rhythmic life. Once we have seen the physiology of respiration in its true light, we are led on all hands to the conclusion that the psyche, in experiencing emotion, is supported by the rhythmic process of breathing, in the same way that, in representation and ideation, it is supported by neural processes. And it will be found that *willing* is supported, in the same way, by the physical processes of metabolism. Here again one must include the innumerable offshoots and ramifications of these processes, which extend throughout the entire organism.

When something is "represented", a neural process takes place, on the basis of which the psyche becomes conscious of its representation; when something is "felt", a modification is effected in the breathing-rhythm, through which a feeling comes to life; and in the same way, when something is "willed", a metabolic process occurs that is the somatic foundation for what the psyche experiences as willing. It should be noted however that it is only in the first case (representation mediated by the nervous system) that the experience is a fully conscious, waking experience. What is mediated through the breathing-rhythm (including in this category everything in the nature of feelings, affects, passions and the like) subsists in normal consciousness with the force only of representations that are dreamed. Willing, with its metabolic succedaneum, is experienced in turn only with that third degree of consciousness, totally dulled, which also persists in sleep. If we look more closely at this series, we shall notice that the experience of willing is in fact wholly different from the experience of representation or ideation. The latter is something like looking at a coloured surface: whereas willing is like looking at a black area in the middle of a coloured field. We see nothing there in the uncoloured part of the surface precisely because — unlike the surrounding part, from which colour impressions are received — no such impressions are at hand from it. We "have the idea" of willing, because within the psyche's field of ideational experience a patch of non-ideation inserts itself, very much as the interruptions of consciousness brought about by sleep insert themselves into the continuum of conscious life. It is to these differing types of conscious apprehension that the soul owes the manifold variety of its experience in ideation, feeling and willing.

There are some noteworthy observations on feeling and willing in Theodor Ziehen's *Manual of Physiological Psychology* — in many ways a standard work within the tradition of current scientific notions concerning the relation between the physical and the psychic. He deals with the relation between the various forms of representation and ideation on the one hand and neural function on the other in a way that is quite in accord with the anthroposophical approach. But when it comes to feeling (see Lecture 9 in his book), he has this to say:

> The older psychology, almost without exception, treats of affects as manifestations of a special, independent faculty. Kant placed the feeling of desire and aversion, as a separate faculty, between those of cognition and appetite, and he expressly emphasised that any further reduction of the three to a common source was impossible. But our previous discussions have shown that feelings of desire and aversion have in fact no such independent evidence; they are not any sounding of the "note of feeling", but simply attributes or signals of sensations and representations.

Here is a theoretical approach which concedes to feeling no independent existence in the life of the soul, seeing it as a mere attribute of ideation. And the result is, it assumes that not only ideation but feeling also is supported by neural processes. The nervous system is thus the somatic element to which the entire psyche is appropriated. Yet the whole basis of this approach amounts to an unnoticed presupposition of the conclusions at which it expects to arrive. It accepts as psychic only what is related to neural processes and then draws the inference that what is not proper to these processes, namely feeling, must be treated as having no independent existence — as a mere signal of ideation.

To abandon this blind alley and return instead to unprejudiced observation of the psyche is to be definitively convinced of the independence of the whole life of feeling. But it is also to appreciate without reserve the actual findings of physiology and at the same time to gain from them the insight that feeling is, as already indicated, peculiar to the breathing-rhythm.

The methodology of natural science denies any sort of existential independence to the will. Unlike feeling, willing is not even a signal of ideation. But this negative assumption, too, is simply based on a prior decision (cf. p. 15 of *Physiological Psychology*) to assign the whole of the psyche to neural process. Yet the plain fact is that what constitutes the peculiar quality of willing cannot really be related to neural process as such. Thus, precisely because of the exemplary clarity with which Ziehen develops the ideas from which he starts, he is forced (as anyone must be) to conclude that analysis of psychic processes in their relation to the life of the body "affords no support to the assumption of a specific faculty of will".

The fact remains that unprejudiced contemplation of the psyche obliges us to recognise the existential independence of the will; and accurate insight into the findings of physiology compels the conclusion that the will, as such, must be linked not with neural but with metabolic processes. If a man wants to form clear concepts in this field, then he must look at the findings of physiology and psychology in the light of the facts themselves, and not, as so often happens in the present-day practice of those sciences, in the light of preconceived opinions and definitions — not to mention theoretical sympathies and antipathies.[2]

---

[2] Compare p. 73 footnote.

Most important of all, he must be able to discern very clearly the mutual interrelation of neural function, breathing-rhythm and metabolic activity respectively. These three forms of activity subsist, not alongside of, but *within* one another. They interpenetrate and enter each other. Metabolic activity is present at all points in the organism; it permeates both the rhythmic organs and the neural ones. But within the rhythmic it is *not* the somatic foundation of feeling, and within the neural it is *not* that of ideation. On the contrary, in both of these fields it is the correlative of will-activity permeating rhythm and permeating the nerves respectively. Only materialistic presupposition can relate the element of *metabolism* in the nerves with the process of ideation. Observation with its roots in reality reports quite differently. It is compelled to recognise that metabolism is present in the nerve to the extent that will is permeating it. And it is the same with the somatic apparatus for rhythm. Everything within that organ that is of the nature of metabolism has to do with the element of will present in it. It is always willing that must be brought into connection with metabolic activity, always feeling that must be related to rhythmic occurrence, irrespective of the particular organ in which metabolism and rhythm are operating.

But in the nerves something else goes on that is quite distinct from metabolism and rhythm. The somatic processes in the nervous system which provide the foundation for representation and ideation are physiologically difficult to grasp. That is because, wherever there is neural function, it is accompanied by the ideation which is ordinary consciousness. But the converse of this is also true. Where there is *no* ideation, there it is never specifically neural function we discern, but only metabolic activity *in* the nerve; or rhythmic occurrence in it, as the case may be. Neurology will never arrive at concepts that measure up to the facts, so long as it fails to see that the specifically *neural* activity of the nerves cannot possibly be an object of physiologically empirical observation. Anatomy and Physiology must bring themselves to recognise that neural function can be located only by a *method of exclusion*. The activity of the nerves is precisely *that* in them which is not perceptible by the senses, though the fact that it must be there can be inferred from what *is* so perceptible, and so can the specific nature of their activity. The only way of representing neural function to ourselves is to see in it those material events, by means of which the purely psycho-spiritual reality of the living *content* of ideation is subdued and devitalised (*herabgelähmt*) to the lifeless representations and ideas we recognise as our ordinary consciousness. Unless this concept finds its way somehow into physiology, physiology can have no hope of explicating neural activity.

At present physiology has committed itself to methods which conceal rather than reveal this concept. And psychology, too, has shut the door in her own face. Look, for instance, at the effects of Herbartian psychology. It confines its attention exclusively to the process of representation, and regards feeling and willing merely as effects consequent on that process. But, for cognition, these "effects" gradually peter out, unless at the same time a candid eye is kept on *actual* feeling and willing; with the result that we are prevented from reaching any valid correlation of feeling and willing with somatic processes. *The body as a whole,* not merely the nervous activity impounded in it, is the physical basis of psychic life. And, just as, for ordinary consciousness, psychic life is naturally classifiable in terms of ideation, feeling and willing, so is physical life classifiable in terms of neural function, rhythmic occurrence and metabolic process.

The question at once arises: in what way do the following enter and inhabit the organism: on the one hand, sense-perception proper, in which neural function merely terminates, and on the other the faculty of motion, which is the effusion of will? Unbiased observation discloses that neither the one nor the other of these *belongs* to the organism in the same sense that neural function, rhythmic occurrence and metabolic process belong to it. What goes on in the senses does not belong immediately to the organism at all. The external world reaches out into the senses, as though they were bays or inlets leading into the organism's own existence. Compassing the processes that take place in the senses, the psyche does not participate in inner organic events; it participates in the extension of outer events into the organism.[3] In the same way, when physical motion is brought about, what we have to do with is not something that is actually situated within the

---

[3] For a critical treatment of this subject see my lecture to the Philosophical Congress at Bologna, 1911.

organism, but an outward working of the organism into the physical equilibrium (or other dynamic relation) between the organism itself and its environment. Within the organism it is only a metabolic process that can be assigned to willing; but the event that is liberated through this process is at the same time an actual happening within the equilibrium, or the dynamics, of the external world. Exerting volition, the life of the psyche overreaches the domain of the organism and combines its action with a happening in the outer world.

The study of the whole matter has been greatly confused by the separation of the nerves into sensory and motor. Securely anchored as this distinction appears to be in contemporary physiological ideas, it is not supported by unbiased observation. The findings of physiology based on neural sections, or on the pathological elimination of certain nerves, do *not* prove what the experiment or the case-history is said to show.[4] They prove something quite different. They prove that the supposed distinction between sensory and motor nerves does not exist. On the contrary, both kinds of nerve are essentially alike. The so-called motor nerve does *not* implement movement in the manner that the theory of two kinds of nerve assumes. What happens is that the nerve *as carrier of the neural function* implements an inner perception of the particular metabolic process that underlies the will — in exactly the same way that the sensory nerve implements perception of what is coming

---

[4] Compare p. 73 footnote.

to pass within the sense-organ. Unless and until neurological theory begins to operate in this domain with clear concepts, no satisfactory co-ordination of psychic and somatic life can come about.[5]

---

[5] In September 1954, forty-seven years after the above words were written, Dr. J. A. V. Bates of the Neurological Research Unit (National Hospital) read his paper, *Can Voluntary Movement be Localized in the Cerebral Cortex?* to a meeting of the British Association at Oxford. He began by demonstrating, on a number of technical grounds, that the inferences drawn from certain well-known facts of observation are not valid inferences, since those facts do not prove that the so-called motor nerve implements movement in the manner that the theory of two kinds of nerve fibre assumes. We should, he suggested, "cease to regard the cortico-spinal tract as an efferent tract from an area where movements are represented and regard it instead as an afferent tract to a region where they are represented"; and he drew attention to the fact that a similar interpretation of the *then* observed facts had been brought forward by Francois Franck as long ago as 1886 but had been rejected in favour of Ferrier's hypothesis of efferent and afferent nerve-fibres. See also *Observations on the Excitable Cortex in Man* by J. A. V. Bates ("Lectures on the Scientific Basis of Medicine" Volume V:1955-56).

While engaged on this translation, I ventured to write to the author to enquire after the subsequent fate of what was clearly an attempt (to quote from this section) to "look at the findings of physiology and psychology in the light of the facts themselves, and not, as so often happens in the present-day practice of those sciences, in the light of preconceived opinions and definitions..." I gather from him that it has neither been answered on the one hand, nor accepted on the other. It appears in fact to have been, at least explicitly, ignored — as (with the possible exception of pure physics) is evidently the normal practice with scientific interpretations or hypotheses, however well supported experimentally, that are radical enough to interfere with theories so long accepted as to have become embodied in definitions. In his obliging reply to my letter Dr. Bates put the present position as follows:

"I would say that in the last fifteen years what I referred to as the classical hypothesis has come to be held with far less conviction by most of those who are researching in the field, but that it is still taught in text books, and will remain a seductive hypothesis for the beginner, I'm afraid, for many years." – *Editor*

* * *

Just as it is possible, psycho-physiologically, to pursue the interrelations between psychic and somatic life which come about in ideation, feeling and willing, in a similar way it is possible, by anthroposophical method, to investigate that relation which the psychic element in ordinary consciousness bears to the spiritual. Applying these methods, the nature of which I have described here and elsewhere, we find that, while representation, or ideation, has a basis in the body in the shape of neural activity or function, it also has a basis in the spiritual. In the other direction — the direction away from the body — the soul stands in relation to a noetically real, which is the basis for the ideation that is characteristic of ordinary consciousness. But this noetic reality can only be experienced through imaginal cognition. And it is so experienced in so far as its content discloses itself to contemplation in the form of coherently linked (*gegliederte*) imaginations. Just as, in the direction of the body, representation rests on the activity of the nerves, so from the other direction does it issue from a noetic reality, which discloses itself in the form of imaginations.

It is this noetic, or spiritual, component of the organism which I have termed in my writings the etheric or life-body. And in doing so I invariably point out that the term "body" is no more vulnerable to objection than the other term "ether"; because my exposition clearly shows that neither of them is predicated materially. This life-body (elsewhere I have also sometimes used the expression "formative-forces body") is that phase of the spiritual, whence the representational life of ordinary consciousness, beginning with birth — or, say, conception — and ending with death, continuously originates.

The feeling-component of ordinary consciousness rests, on the bodily side, on rhythmic occurrence. From the spiritual side it streams from a level of spiritual reality that is investigated, in anthroposophical research, by methods which I have, in my writings, designated as inspirational. (Here again it is emphasised that I employ this term solely with the meaning I have given it in my own descriptions; it is not to be equated with inspiration in the colloquial sense.) In the spiritual reality that lies at the base of the soul and is apprehensible though inspiration there is disclosed that phase of the spiritual, proper to the human being, which extends beyond birth and death. It is in this field that anthroposophy brings its spiritual investigations to bear on the problem of immortality. *As the mortal part of the sentient human being manifests itself through rhythmic occurrences in the body, so does the immortal spirit-kernel of the soul reveal itself in the inspiration-content of intuitive consciousness.*

For such an intuitive consciousness the will, which depends, in the somatic direction, on metabolic processes, issues forth from the spirit through what in my writings I have termed authentic intuitions. What is, from one point of view, the "lowest" somatic activity (metabolism) is correlative to a spiritually highest one. Hence, ideation, which relies on neural activity, achieves something like a perfection of somatic manifestation; while the bodily processes associated with willing are only a feeble reflection of willing. The real representation is *alive*, but, as somatically conditioned, it is subdued and deadened. The content remains the same. Real willing, on the other hand, whether or no it finds an outcome in the physical world, takes its course in regions that are accessible only to intuitive vision; its somatic correlative has almost nothing to do with its content. It is at this level of spiritual reality, disclosed to intuition, that we find influences from previous terrestrial lives at work in later ones. And it is in this kind of context that anthroposophy approaches the problems of repeated lives and of destiny. As the body fulfils its life in neural function, rhythmic occurrence and metabolic process, so the human spirit discloses its life in all that becomes apparent in imaginations, inspirations and intuitions. The body, within its own field, affords participation in *its* external world in two directions, in sensuous happenings and in motor happenings; and so does the spirit — in so far as that experiences the representations of the psyche *imaginally* (even in ordinary consciousness) from the one direction, while in the other — in willing — it in-forms the *intuitive* impulses that are realising themselves through metabolic processes. Looking towards the body, we find neural activity that is taking the form of representation-experience, ideation; looking towards the spirit, we realise the spirit-content of the imagination that is flowing into precisely that ideation.

Brentano was primarily sensitive to the noetic side of the psyche's experience in representation. That is why he characterises this experience as figurative, i.e. as an imaginal event. Yet when it is not only the private content of the soul that is being experienced, but also a somewhat that demands judgmental acknowledgment or repudiation, then there is added to the representation a soul experience deriving from spirit. The content of this experience remains "unconscious" in the ordinary sense, because it consists of imaginations of a spiritual that existentially underpins the physical object. These imaginations add nothing to the representation *except that its content exists*. Hence Brentano's diremption of *mere representation* (which imaginally experiences merely an inwardly present) from judgment (which imaginally experiences an externally given; but which is aware of that experience only as existential acknowledgment or repudiation).

When it comes to *feeling*, Brentano has no eyes for its somatic basis in rhythmic occurrence; instead he limits his field of observation to love and hate; that is, to vestiges, in the sphere of ordinary consciousness, of inspirations which themselves remain unconscious. Lastly the *will* is outside his purview altogether; because he is determined to direct his gaze only to phenomena *within the psyche*; and because there is something in the will that is *not* encapsulated in the soul, but of which the soul avails itself in order to participate in the outside world. Brentano's divisive classification of psychological phenomena may therefore be characterised as follows: he takes his stand at a vantage-point which is truly illuminating, but is only so if the eye is focused on the spirit-kernel of the soul — and yet he insists on aiming from there at the phenomena of ordinary everyday consciousness.[6]

---

[6] The Section concludes with a remark that these observations are intended as supplementary to a passage in the memorial address on Brentano, which constitutes Chapter III of *Von Seelenrätseln*. The passage is on page 90.

VIII

THE REAL BASIS OF INTENTIONAL RELATION

IN BRENTANO'S PSYCHOLOGY, the "intentional relation" is treated *simply as a fact* of ordinary consciousness. It is a psychic fact; but no attempt is made to clarify further by showing how that fact is articulated into the whole psychic experience. Perhaps I may be permitted, in bare outline, to advance a corollary to it on the basis of my own systematic and extensive observations. These latter really call for presentation in much greater detail and with all the supporting evidence. But up to now circumstances have made it impossible for me to go beyond introducing them cursorily into oral lectures; and what I can add here is still only a brief outline statement of the *results*. I invite the reader to entertain them provisionally on that footing. At the same time they are not put forward merely as hazarded "insights", but rather as something I have striven year in and year out to establish with the means that modern science makes available.

In the particular psychic experience which Brentano denotes by the term *judgment*[1] there is added to the mere representation (which consists in the formation of an inner image) an acknowledgment or repudiation of the image. The question that arises for the psychologist is: *What exactly is it, within the psyche's experience, wherethrough is brought about not merely the presented image "green tree", but also the judgment "there is a green tree"?* This

---
[1] See Introduction p. 11.

somewhat cannot be located within the rather circumscribed area of representational activity that is assigned to ordinary consciousness. (In the second volume of my *Riddles of Philosophy* [*Die Rätsel der Philosophie*], in the section entitled "The World as Illusion", I gave some account of the various epistemological ideas to which this difficulty has given rise.) We have to do with an experience that lies outside that area. The problem is to find its "where". Where, when the human being confronts a sense-object in the act of perception, is this "somewhat" to be looked for? Not in anything he so receives in the process of perception, that the receiving can be understood through any physiological or psychological ideas that posit outer object on one side and immediate sensation on the other. When someone has the visual perception "green tree", the fact of the judgment "there is a green tree" is not to be found in that relation between "tree" and "eye" which is viable to either physiological or psychological explication. The experience had by the psyche, which amounts to this inner fact of *judgment*, is an additional relation between "man" and "tree" strictly other than the bare relation between "tree" and "eye". Yet it is only this latter relation that is fully and sharply experienced in ordinary-level consciousness. The former relation remains a dull, subconscious one, which only comes to light in its *product* — namely the *acknowledgment* of the "green tree" as an existent. In every perception that reaches the point of a "judgment" we have a *double* relation to objectivity.

It is only possible to gain insight into this double relation, if the prevailing fragmentary doctrine of the senses is replaced by an exhaustive one. If we take into account the whole of what is relevant in assigning the characteristics of a human sense, we shall find we must allow the name "senses" to more than is usually so labeled. That which constitutes the "eye", for example, a "sense" is also present when we experience the fact: *another "I" is being observed*, or: *the thought of another human being is being recognised as such*. The mistake usually made, in the face of such facts as these, is failure to maintain a certain very valid and necessary distinction. As an instance of this, people imagine that, when they hear somebody else's words, "sense" only comes in to the extent that "hearing" as such is involved, and that all the rest is assignable to an inner, non-sensory activity. But that is not the case. In the hearing of human words and in the understanding of them as thoughts a threefold activity is involved, and each component of this threefold activity requires separate consideration, if we mean to conceptualise in a scientifically valid way. One of these activities is "hearing". But "hearing" *per se* is no more a "becoming aware of words" than "touching" is a "seeing". And just as it is proper to distinguish the sense of "touch" from that of "sight", so is it to distinguish the sense of "hearing" from that of "being aware of words", and again from that of "comprehending thoughts". A starveling psychology and a starveling epistemology both follow as consequences from the failure to sharply distinguish the "comprehending of thoughts" from the activity of thinking, and to recognise the "sense" character of the former process. The only reason for our common failure to distinguish is, that the organ of "being aware of words" and that of "comprehending thoughts" are neither of them outwardly perceptible like the ear, which is the organ of "hearing". Actually there are "organs" for both these perceptual activities, just as, for "hearing", there is the ear.

If, scrutinising them without omissions, one carries the findings of physiology and psychology through to their logical conclusion, one will arrive at the following view of human sensory organisation. We have to distinguish: The sense for *perceiving the "I" of the other human being*; the sense for *comprehending thoughts*; the sense for *being aware of words*; the sense of hearing; the sense of warmth; the sense of sight; the sense of taste; the sense of balance (the perceptual experience, that is, of oneself as being in a certain equilibrium with the outer world); the sense of movement (the perceptual experiencing of the stillness or the motion of one's own limbs or, alternatively, of one's own stillness or motion by contrast with the outer world); the sense of life (experience of being situated within an organism — feeling of subjective self-awareness); and the sense of touch. All these senses bear the distinguishing marks by virtue whereof we properly call "eye" and "ear" by the name of "senses".

To ignore the validity of such distinctions is to import disorder into the whole relation between our knowledge and reality. It is to suffer the ignominious burden of ideas that cut us off from experiencing the actual. For instance, if a man calls the "eye" a "sense" and refuses to accept any "sense" for "being aware of words", then the idea which that man forms of the "eye" remains an unreal fancy.

I am persuaded that Fritz Mauthner in his brilliant way speaks, in his linguistic works, of a "happening-sense" (*Zufallssinnen*) only because he has in view a too fragmentary doctrine of the senses. If it were not for that, he would detect how a "sense" inserts itself into "reality". In practice, when a human being confronts a sensory object, it is never through *one* sense that he acquires an impression, but always, in addition, through at least one other of those just enumerated. The relation to one particular sense enters ordinary-level consciousness with especial sharpness; while the other remains *more obtuse*. But the senses also differ from one another in a further respect: some of them afford a relation to the outer world that is experienced more as external nexus; the others more one that is bound up very intimately with our own being. Senses that are most intimately bound up with our own being are (for example) the sense of equilibrium, the sense of motion, the sense of life — and also of course the sense of touch. When there is perception by these senses of the outer world, it is always obscurely accompanied by experience of the percipient's own being. You can even say that in their case a certain obtuseness of conscious percipience obtains, precisely because the element in it of external relationship is shouted down *by* the experience of our own being. For instance: a physical object is *seen*, and at the same time the sense of equilibrium furnishes an impression. What is seen is sharply perceived. This "seen" leads to representation of a physical object. The experience through the sense of equilibrium remains, *qua* perception, dull and obtuse; but it comes to life in the judgment: "That which is seen exists" or "There is a thing seen". Natures are not, in reality, juxtaposed to one another in abstract mutual exclusion; they, together with their distinguishing marks, overlap and interpenetrate. Hence, in the whole gamut of the "senses" there are some that mediate relation to the outer world rather less and the experience of one's own being rather more. These latter are sunken further into the inner life of the psyche than, for example, eye and ear; and, for that reason, their perceptual function manifests as inner psychic experience. But one must still distinguish, even in their case, the properly psychic from the perceptual element, just as in the case of, say, seeing one distinguishes the outer event or object from the inner psychic experience evoked with it.

For those who adopt the anthroposophical standpoint, there can be no shirking of refined notional distinctions of this kind. They must be capable of distinguishing "awareness of words" from hearing, in one direction; and of distinguishing, in the other, this "awareness of words" from the "understanding of words" brought about by one's own intellection; just as ordinary consciousness distinguishes between a tree and a lump of rock. If this were less frequently ignored, it would be recognised that anthroposophy has two aspects; not only the one that people usually dub "mystical", but also the other one, the one that conduces to investigations not less scientific than those of natural science, but in fact more scientific, since they necessitate a more refined and methodical habit of conceptualisation than even ordinary philosophy does. I suspect that Wilhelm Dilthey[2] was tending, in his philosophical enquiries, towards the doctrine I have outlined here concerning the senses; but that he was unable to achieve his purpose because he never reached the point of sufficiently elaborating the requisite ideas.

---

[2] Compare the author's *Die Rätsel der Philosophie*, 8th Edition.

BIBLIOGRAPHY

(Compiled in 1970 and now outdated)

Note: GA = *Gesamtausgabe* (Complete Edition), published by Verlag der Rudolf Steiner Nachlassverwaltung, Dornach, Switzerland; the preceding number (e.g. "No. 20GA") is the serial number in the Bibliographical Survey thereof.

The Philosophy of Freedom, 7th edition, translated by Michael Wilson, Rudolf Steiner Press, 1964. (Also published as *The Philosophy of Spiritual Activity*.)

Goethe's Theory of Knowledge, 2nd edition, published with the title *A Theory of Knowledge based on Goethe's World Conception*, Anthroposophic Press, U.S.A., 1969.

Truth and Science, published with the title *Truth and Knowledge*, as Part II, in *The Philosophy of Spiritual Activity*, translated by Rita Stebbing, Rudolf Steiner Publications Inc., New York, 1963.

Von Menschenrätsel, 4th edition, 1957, N. 20 GA. Not translated into English.

Knowledge of the Higher Worlds. How is it achieved? Revised edition by D.S.O., C.D., A.B., Rudolf Steiner Press, 1969.

Occult Science — an Outline, translated by George and Mary Adams, Rudolf Steiner Press, 1962/3.

Die Rätsel der Philosophie in ihrer Geschichte als Umriss dargestellt, 8th edition, 1968, No. 18 GA. English translation in preparation in U.S.A.

The title of the lecture given to the Philosophical Congress at Bologna in April 1911 (see p.71), was: *Die psychologischen Grundlagen und die erkenntnistheorische Stellung der Theosophie.* Not translated into English. Text is contained in the volume entitled: *Philosophie und Anthroposophie. Gesammelte Aufsätze 1904-1918,* No. 35 GA.

INDEX

ABSTRACTION, 53–56, 58
Adams, G., 14
Alchemy, 2
Anatomy, 70
'Anthropology':
  meaning of in this book, 20–21
'Anthroposophie', 20n
Aristotle (Aristotelian), 6, 15, 54
Astrology, 2
Astronomy, 2
Augustine, Saint, 15

BATES, J. A. V., 73n
'Benumbing':
  of unconscious life a condition of consciousness, 33–35, 53–55, 70, 76
Birth, 75
Blake, W., 15
Boehme, J., 14, 15
Boundaries of Cognition, see Science, limits of
Brain, the, 49–51, 65
Breathing, 64–78

Bruno, Giordano, 15
Brown, N. O., 8

COLERIDGE, S. T., 3–4, 5, 16, 21n
Concepts, 4, 21, 53–56, 58
Cusanus, (Nicolas of Cusa), 15

DEATH, 74–75
  relation of to intellect and consciousness, 4, 32–34 (see also Benumbing)
Descartes, R., 1, 3–5, 24
Dessoir, M., 11–12, 19
Destiny, 76
Dilthey, W., 85
Dreaming:
  and Sleeping as modes of normal daytime consciousness, 23, 25, 45–46, 66
Du Bois-Reymond, 27

ELEMENTS, 15
Etheric Body, 47–48, 74–75

INDEX

Existential Judgments, 9ff, 77, 79–80
Existentialism, 9–11
Experiments, psychological, 59–61
Expression, of noetic experience, 35–36

FEELING, 64–78
Fichte, J. G., 50
Franck, F., 73n

GOETHE, 10, 21, and 21n, 35
Grene, M., 4

HALLUCINATION, 46–47
Harvey, W., 14
Hegel, G. H. W., 49
Heidegger, M., 8
Herbartian psychology, 20n, 70
Hermetism, 15
Humours, 15
Husserl, E., 9–10

IMAGES, 4
Imaginal cognition, 34–36, 74, 77

Inspirational cognition, 75
Intellect, 4
Intentionality, 10–11, 23–25, 79–85
Intuition, and Intuitive consciousness, 25–26, 36, 55–56, 61, 75–76

JAMES, W., 23–26
Judgment(s), 4, 9–11, 27–28, 79–81 (see also *Existential Judgments*)

KANT, 11, 67
Knauer, V., 53

LIFE-BODY (see *Etheric Body*)
Logic, 37–38, 45–46

MACH, E., 25
Matter, 1, 53–55
Mauthner, F., 83
Mediumship, 46
Memory:
  used to illustrate experience of spiritual perception, 42–44
  contrasted therewith, 57–58

cannot retain spiritual
perceptions, 57
Metabolism, 65–78
Mirror, relation of
conscious to unconscious
mind compared with,
13
Music, experience of,
64–65

NATURE, 4ff, 49–50
Neo-Platonism, 15
Nerves and Nervous system,
64–78
'sensory' and 'motor',
72–73, 73n
Neurology, 4, 14, 72–73,
73n
Nominalism, 53

OCCULT:
defined, 5
qualities, 1, 5
science, 3, 5
Organs of Spirit, 21–22,
21n, 22n, 26–36, 55

PHENOMENOLOGY, 9–10
Physiology, 63–78, 82
Platonism, 15

Polanyi, M., 5, 8
Popper, K., 8
Proofs, of spiritual
perception, 59–61

QUALITIES:
occult, 1–2, 5
physical, 3, 11, 17

REALISM, 53
Representation(s), 30–35,
42–48, 63–73
imaginal, 34–36, 74–75,
76–77
Rhythm and Rhythmic
process, 64–66
Russell, B., 7

SCIENCE, 1–2, 12, 14,
63–64, 68
limits of, 6–8, 27–29,
49–52
Scientific impulse, the, 6–8
Scientific Revolution, the,
1ff, 14–16
Senses and Sense-perception,
1, 19–30, 33–38, 42–44,
57, 64, 71–74, 80–85
Sleeping (see Dreaming)
Spicker, G., 7, 51

Spiritual organs (see *Organs of Spirit*)
Spiritual science, 3

TRI-UNITY, 13, 15, 63–78

UNCONSCIOUS, relation of to conscious mind, 13

VIGILANCE, required for spiritual perception, 23–25
Vischer, F. T., 7, 49–50
Volkelt, J., 49

WILL, 44–47, 65–78
awareness of, 66

ZIEHEN, T., 45, 66–68
Zimmermann, R., 20n

SELECTED WORKS BY OWEN BARFIELD

First published

Books by Owen Barfield

The Silver Trumpet	1925
History in English Words	1926
Poetic Diction: A Study in Meaning	1928
Romanticism Comes of Age	1944
This Ever Diverse Pair	1950
Saving the Appearances: A Study in Idolatry	1957
Worlds Apart: A Dialogue of the 1960's	1963
Unancestral Voice	1965
Speaker's Meaning	1967
What Coleridge Thought	1971
The Rediscovery of Meaning and Other Essays	1977
History, Guilt and Habit	1979
Orpheus: A Poetic Drama	1983 (written 1937)
Owen Barfield on CS Lewis	1989
Night Operation	2008 (written 1975)
Eager Spring	2008 (written 1988)
The Rose on the Ash-Heap	2009 (written 1929)

Translations and edited works of Rudolf Steiner

World Economy: The Formation of a Science of World-Economics (trans. with T. Gordon-Jones)	1936
Anthroposophy: An Introduction	1961
The Case for Anthroposophy	1970
Guidance in Esoteric Training (trans. with Charles Davy)	1972
The Year Participated: being Rudolf Steiner's *Calendar of the Soul* translated and paraphrased for an English ear	1985

Edited works by other authors

Man and Animal: Their Essential Differences, by Hermann Poppelbaum	1960
The Voice of Cecil Harwood	1979

www.ingramcontent.com/pod-product-compliance
Lightning Source LLC
Chambersburg PA
CBHW032050090426
42744CB00004B/146